CRUISING GUIDE TO

Text and charts by
Chris Doyle
Updated by
Jeff Fisher
with Carnival by
Cathy Winn
Illustrations
Sally Erdle

Photos by:
Jeff Fisher
Roger Neckels
Chris Doyle
Virginia Barlow
Carnival photos by:
Photo Sunny

PUBLISHED BY

CHRIS DOYLE PUBLISHING
in association with
CRUISING GUIDE PUBLICATIONS

ISBN 0-944428-37-1

Published 1996

DISTRIBUTION

USA AND WORLDWIDE
Cruising Guide Publications, P.O. Box 1017
Dunedin, Florida 34697-1017
Tel: 813-733-5322 Fax: 813-734-8179
orders only: 800-330-9542

TRINIDAD AND TOBAGO
Jack Dausend
Dausend Enterprises
81 Apple Blossom Ave.,
Petit Valley
Diego Martin
Tel/Fax: 632-0724

ST. VINCENT & THE GRENADINES
Frances Punnett, Box 17, St. Vincent, W. I.
Tel: 809-458-4246 Fax: 809-456-2620

ST. LUCIA
Cecil Baptiste, Box 1457, Castries
Tel: 809-452-0823

GRENADA
Tikal, Box 51, Young St., St. George's
Tel: 809-440-2310

USING THIS BOOK

In the text we give a very rough price guide to the restaurants. This is an idea of what you might spend to eat out and have a drink per person. Our guide runs as follows:

(A) is $50 U.S. or over
(B) is $25 to $50 U.S.
(C) is $12 to $25 U.S.
(D) is under $12 U.S.

We use the following abbreviations:

F = Facsimile   T = Telephone

In our sketch charts the main shoal areas are marked with a broken line and major reefs and rocks with crosses.

These areas are colored yellow on the sketch charts.

They have been drawn for yachts drawing up to about 6.5 feet of water. Those navigating deeper draft yachts will have to refer to the depths on their charts. We occasionally draw a line round an area which is relatively shallow, though deep enough to navigate over. We do this to make it stand out. In such cases we leave this area blue like the surrounding water.

Compass roses point to true north, but where we give bearings they are magnetic.

Latitude and longitude, where given, were taken by GPS using a Garmin 50 set on WGS 84 map datum.

We are happy to accept advertising. Advertising enables us to update regularly and to include color photography and color charts. If you wish to help us keep it that way, tell everyone you do business with "I read about it in the Cruising Guide" It helps us no end.

If you would like to tell us about your experiences, good or bad, we will consider your comments when writing the next edition.

Also if you would like give us new information it helps steer us in the right direction next time we update the guide. Send your comments to:

Jeff Fisher,
Box 51,
Young St.,
St. George's
Grenada
T&F: 809-440-2556

NOTICE

The information in this guide was correct to the best of our knowledge at the time of going to press.

No warranty, expressed or implied, is made by the publishers for any errors or omissions in this publication. The skipper must use this guide together with proper charts and other navigational aids and not place undue credence in the accuracy of this guide. This guide should not be used for navigation.

AUTHOR'S ACKNOWLEDGMENTS

Writing this guide would have been impossible without a great deal of help. So many people gave us information and help that it would be impossible to mention them all.

We would particularly like to thank Don Stollmeyer at Power Boats, Anne Farfan at YSATT and Katrina Kelshall at TIDCO for helping us with information.

CRUISING
GUIDE
TO
TRINIDAD
AND TOBAGO

Trinidad was part of South America as recently as 10,000 years ago and geographically more closely resembles Venezuela than the rest of the Caribbean. While it lacks those perfectly peaceful anchorages backed by powdery palm-fringed beaches which typify the other islands, it offers a rich cultural heritage and an amazing wealth of natural wildlife unseen in the islands to the north. Tobago by contrast is a typically idyllic Caribbean island that runs at a gentle pace under swaying palms, with the added bonus of a much larger diversity of birds than can be found in the islands to the north.

Trinidad and Tobago are now a favorite destination for cruising sailors. Strangely enough, a few years ago, yachts rarely visited these islands. It was felt that Tobago was too far to the east and hard to get to and most yachtspeople thought there was nothing for them in Trinidad.

Attitudes began to change when Don Stollmeyer, the manager of a yard called Power Boats, decided to invest in a used 50-ton travel lift. The only way to justify it was to expand into hauling visiting yachts. Within just a few years this had grown into a thriving industry of hauling and repairing yachts involving many yards and hundreds of people.

It also put Trinidad and Tobago on the map for cruising folk who came to haul out but stayed to discover another side of Trinidad; an island whose exotic and flamboyant nature includes rain forests and swamps with monkeys, parrots, macaws, manatees and giant leatherback turtles. They discovered too, one of the most fun-loving and hospitable people in the Caribbean whose carnival is considered by many to be the best in the world. When the fun got too much, they found, as Trinidadians have long known, that a week or two in Tobago is the perfect way to relax.

Few nations offer such diverse attractions in such a small area.

Welcome to Trinidad and Tobago!

INTRODUCTION

TABLE OF CONTENTS

OLD BOOK ILLUSTRATION

CRUISING INFORMATION

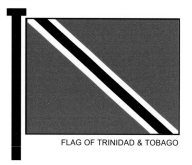

FLAG OF TRINIDAD & TOBAGO

Cruising comfort

The wind often dies at night in Trinidad. This can make it warm for sleeping below, especially in marinas. Windscoops or efficient 12 volt fans are useful luxuries. Those planning to spend long periods in marinas might find a small air conditioning unit worthwhile. These can be rented locally.

Fishing

Fishing is excellent throughout this region. The westerly setting equatorial current hits the continental shelf, causing colder nutrient rich water to rise from the sea bed. That old lure and line that has been hanging unsuccessfully over the stern of your yacht for hundreds of miles is likely to jump into action and surprise you.

From our questioning of locals it appears that ciguatera poisoning is extremely rare in Trinidad and Tobago. However, to ensure your own safety, avoid really big barracudas, Spanish mackerel and jacks.

Swimming

While the water in Trinidad is often colored by run-off from the Orinoco it is perfectly good for swimming and there is also good snorkeling in some anchorages, although the visibility is restricted. The small caimans found mainly in inland lakes and reservoirs and brackish estuaries are not considered dangerous, unless molested.

Money Matters

Currency is the TT dollar which varies in value to the US and you currently get 5 to 6 TT dollars for one US. US dollars are widely accepted and easily changed into local currencies. EC dollars can also be changed in the banks though the rate of exchange is not very favorable.

Travelers checks are excellent and credit cards work well.

Language

English is the language of Trinidad and Tobago, which makes it easy for many of us.

Photography

Photographic supplies are easily available in the large towns in Trinidad. Film is usually reasonably priced. There are first rate facilities for developing and printing your print film. Slide film can also be developed fast and well but it has to be the E6 process type (Fujichrome, Ektachrome). For aquatic shots a polarizing filter brings out the water colors.

Medical care

You can get good medical and dental care in Trinidad and Tobago. There are many doctors and modern facilities. For a current list of doctors check the latest Trinidad and Tobago Boater's Directory (usually given free when you clear in). The St. Clair medical Center (T:628-1451/2/8615) is a private establishment which will take care of most of your needs. You could also visit the Mount Hope Medical Sciences Complex (T:645-4673/2640) or the Community Hospital of Seventh Day Adventists (T:622-1191/2). If you need an ambulance in an emergency you could try calling the coast guard for help on the VHF.

Trinidad has a very rich wildlife which includes poisonous snakes like the fer-de-lance, bushmaster and coral snake. There are also scorpions and centipedes. Most of these exist in the wilder regions. They don't present much danger as long as you keep your eyes open and tread carefully. Small ticks and biting insects can be more annoying. The liberal use of repellent or long pants and shoes and socks is advisable when you go exploring in the forest. Insect repellent can also be handy ashore in the evenings.

If you have not yet learnt to identify the poisonous manchineel tree, get someone to show you one. These pretty trees grow close to the water and the sap is highly toxic as are their little green apples. It can be dangerous to shelter under one in the rain, and a fire made from manchineel sticks produces toxic smoke.

Drugs

Illegal drugs are taken very seriously by law enforcement officers throughout this area. Anyone getting caught even with one joint can expect confiscation of the yacht, a monster fine and a long jail term.

Security

Trinidad is a bustling and exotic country, bursting with activity, and among other life forms there is a light-fingered brigade and there are also those who rob with guns. Illegal drugs exist in Trinidad and have certainly been linked to some of the crimes. As to theft from yachts we have been surprisingly lucky so far. There have only been a few break-ins, and occasional items stolen from yachts in the yards.

However, it is sensible to take a few precautions. Do not keep large quantities of cash either on board or on your person. Use credit cards and travellers checks as much as possible, as they are insured. Keep your dinghy locked up, especially at night. If you have anything of special value on your boat hide it really well.

Be streetwise ashore. Stay aware of what is going on around you. Don't set your handbag or brief case down somewhere and move away. If you are renting a car, do not leave anything valuable, even in the trunk. It is also advisable to use a wheel locking device if it is supplied.

Before walking or jogging on your own ask local advice on the safety of the area concerned.

WEATHER

The weather is generally pleasant, with temperatures of 78-85° Fahrenheit year round. There are two seasons, the rainy season (June to December) and the dry season (January to May). These vary from year to year and the starting and finishing times are not exact. During the rainy season Trinidad is considerably wetter than Tobago or the islands to the north, though there are still many pleasant days and lots of sunshine.

Tobago lies in the regular trade wind belt and you usually have a good breeze. The weather along the coast of Trinidad is more variable. Winds often intensify during daylight hours and calm down at night. Many yachts heading from Trinidad to Tobago power overnight in the calm. This rule is not cast in stone and it is less likely to be calm at night when the trades are blowing hard.

A westerly to northwesterly setting current flows past Tobago and along the north coast of Trinidad. It rushes between Trinidad and Tobago. When close to Trinidad, you can sometimes keep out of the current by staying within a mile or two of the mainland coast.

Trinidad is considered to be below the hurricane belt which is why many people leave their yachts here during the summer. However, Tobago has had a few hurricanes. It is sensible to listen to the weather, not only because of hurricanes, but because easterly waves and other disturbances can come through with a lot of rain and wind.

Should a storm threaten, you should go to a secure harbor. In Tobago the Bon Accord lagoon is the only safe harbor, so if you draw 6 feet or more be prepared to sail to Trinidad or Grenada. In Trinidad the fishing harbor south of Port of Spain is probably as good a place as any.

The anchorage in Chaguaramas can be rolly during periods of southerly winds. Very rarely such a wind will reach proportions that make it dangerous to be tied to the docks in Power Boats or Peake, and dinghies can get smashed, particularly in Power Boats. CrewsInn and Stella Maris and other facilities right up in the eastern corner are generally protected.

While this area is too far south to be subject to northers, the swells from these systems do affect the area, creating uncomfortable seas and rolly anchorages in the harbors along the northern coasts of Trinidad and Tobago.

Weather forecasts

Trinidad and Tobago have several radio stations both on the AM and FM bands. Gem Radio on 93.5 Mhz FM gives forecasts from the Miami weather bureau following the news every hour on the hour from 0600-1800.

For some while there has been an informal VHF net at 0800 on channel 68. One of its better features is the weather forecast. North Post radio also gives weather on 0940 and 1640 or by special request. They stand by on VHF:16 and switch to 25, 26, 27, 28 or 78.

Those who have ham or SSB radios will be interested to know that the Antilles Emergency and Weather net is on 3815 kHz at 0635 AST and on LSB 7163 KHZ at 1840. This gives weather and emergency information. The Caribbean Weather net is on 4003 kHz at 0815 (all times local) and 8104 kHz at 0830. There is also a broadcast on 8107 kHz at 1815, but only when there is a warning.

NAVIGATION

Tides

The tidal range in Trinidad and Tobago is around 3 feet, which is significantly greater than in the Windwards and Leewards. Currents vary with the tides, and along the north coast you can expect some kind of an east going tide from one hour before low water till about two hours before high water.

Lights

Major lights in Trinidad and Tobago are generally reliable. In particular the light on Chacachacare Island is a big help to those sailing to Trinidad. The light at Fort George in Scarborough is also reliable, though I would not advise approaching Tobago at night because of the shoals and strong currents. Don't rely on smaller lights marked on navigation charts, some of these have been taken out.

Buoys

The whole area comes under the IALA B system (red right returning). However, buoys are not always in place so treat them with caution.

Fishing Boats

Night sailing along the north coast of Trinidad requires great caution. Small fish-

GPS POSITIONS - as taken with a Garmin-50 on WGS-84 - for planning

PLACE	LAT (NORTH) deg mins	LONG (WEST) deg mins
Trinidad		
Approach to Boca de Monos	10 43.7	61 40.1
Chacachacare I.	10 40.5	61 43.9
Chaguaramas	10 40.7	61 38.4
La Vache Bay	10 46.1	61 29.0
Maracas Bay	10 46.8	61 25.6
Monos I., Grand Fond Bay	10 41.0	61 40.8
Monos I., Morris Bay	10 41.5	61 40.6
Pointe-A-Pierre	10 19.9	61 28.4
Scotland Bay	10 41.9	61 40.1
Trinidad and & Tobago Yacht Club	10 40.5	61 34.0
Winns Bay, Gaspar Grande I.	10 39.4	61 39.7
Tobago		
Bon Accord Lagoon, channel entrance	11 11.3	60 50.6
Bulldog Shoal	11 08.8	60 44.5
Castara Bay	11 16.5	60 42.2
Charlotteville	11 19.8	60 33.4
Englishman's Bay	11 17.7	60 40.6
King's Bay	11 15.5	60 32.9
Little Tobago, off the northwest point	11 18.4	60 30.6
Mt. Irvine Bay	11 11.5	60 48.3
Parlatuvier Bay	11 18.2	60 39.3
Pigeon Point	11 10.0	60 50.9
Plymouth	11 12.7	60 46.8
Scarborough	11 10.6	60 44.2

MILEAGE CHART

This table is approximate and is offered as a guide to planning.
Distances sailed vary greatly due to wind and current.

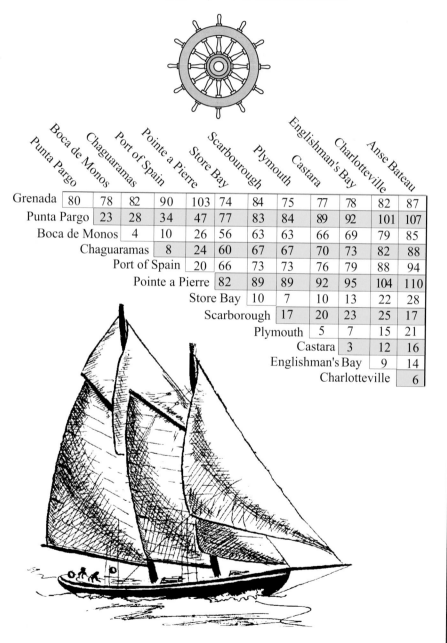

	Punta Pargo	Boca de Monos	Chaguaramas	Port of Spain	Pointe a Pierre	Store Bay	Scarborough	Plymouth	Castara	Englishman's Bay	Charlotteville	Anse Bateau
Grenada	80	78	82	90	103	74	84	75	77	78	82	87
Punta Pargo		23	28	34	47	77	83	84	89	92	101	107
Boca de Monos			4	10	26	56	63	63	66	69	79	85
Chaguaramas				8	24	60	67	67	70	73	82	88
Port of Spain					20	66	73	73	76	79	88	94
Pointe a Pierre						82	89	89	92	95	104	110
Store Bay							10	7	10	13	22	28
Scarborough								17	20	23	25	17
Plymouth									5	7	15	21
Castara										3	12	16
Englishman's Bay											9	14
Charlotteville												6

ing boats have no fixed lights, but they will briefly flash a light when they see your yacht coming. Stay well clear of fishing boats whenever you can. Large nets of tough plastic are sometimes set, which could ensnare your yacht.

Oil Rigs

In the Gulf of Paria there are several derelict oil rigs left in place and single oil pipes that stick up out of the water. Most of these have lights, but it is far better to sail here during the day when you can keep a good lookout.

CUSTOMS AND IMMIGRATION

Customs and immigration are simple for entering Trinidad or Tobago. If you are a national of Cuba, the USSR and countries that used to be part of the Socialist block or the Dominican Republic, Haiti, India, Iran, Iraq, Jordan, Kuwait, Lebanon, Libya, Nigeria, Papau New Guinea, Saudi Arabia, Sri Lanka, Syria, Tanzania and Uganda you need a visa. Otherwise you do not.

There are two places to clear in, Chaguaramas in Trinidad and Scarborough in Tobago. There is usually someone on duty 24-hours a day and you are required to check in as soon as you arrive. You may want to time your arrival for normal office hours (0800-1600, Monday through Friday, excluding holidays) as you will be charged about $45US overtime outside these hours. There are also reasonable charges which include TT$50 for every 30 days spent in the country. In addition to the above, skippered charter yachts pay a tax of $10 US per passenger. This may be increased to $50US in the near future.

Once you have cleared in you are free to move between anchorages in both Trinidad and Tobago. Should you clear into Trinidad and plan to leave from Tobago (or vice versa) you must notify the immigration officer at the entry port so they can arrange to

18

DURATEC VINYL ESTER PRIMER

FOR OSMOSIS & BLISTER REPAIRS OF COMPOSITE & METAL BOAT BOTTOMS

DURATEC Vinyl Ester Primer is the perfect substrate for anti-fouling bottom, topside, and deck topcoat paint systems. Rapid build-up and sandability greatly reduces repair time versus epoxy fairing and paint systems.

DURATEC Vinyl Ester Primer is a high quality primer manufactured from the finest corrosion-resistant vinyl ester resin system available today. This unique, high-build (up to two millimeters, wet on wet), easily sandable, porosity-free primer can be sprayed, rolled or brushed onto peeled or sanblasted composite surfaces.

Osmosis Damaged Hull

Same boat hull showing DURATEC Vinyl Ester Primer sanded to an 80-grit finish.

MARINE APPLICATIONS
- **OSMOSIS/BLISTER REPAIRS**
- **RAPID SURFACE FAIRING**
- **IN-MOLD AS OSMOSIS/BLISTER BARRIER**

TOOLING APPLICATIONS
- **MOLD SURFACING**
- **MOLD RESURFACING**

NEW PRODUCT
- *VINYL ESTER FAIRING PUTTY*

Also available from Hawkeye Industries:

DURATEC POLYESTER PRIMERS & COATINGS

Full Range of:
HI-BUILD PRIMERS, HI-GLOSS PIGMENTED & CLEAR COATINGS

* MOLD REPAIRS * MOLD RESURFACING * GEL COAT REPAIRS * PATTERN SURFACING * WOOD FINISHES *

HAWKEYE INDUSTRIES, INC.

3050 BROOKVIEW DR.
MARIETTA, GA 30068 USA
PHN (770) 977-3336
FAX (770) 565 5094

DISTRIBUTOR:

Marc One MARINE SUPPLIES LTD.
Specializing in Fibreglass Reinforced Plastics

69 MUCURAPO ROAD, ST. JAMES, TRINIDAD, W.I.
TEL: (809) 622-7926 FAX: (809) 622-1973

get your papers to your port of exit.

Immigration Extensions

Arriving yachtspeople are normally given up to three months. If you wish to stay longer than this you must apply for an extension with the immigration about a week before you need it. There is a fee of around $150TT for this.

Signing crew on or off.

If a crew is leaving or arriving while you are in Trinidad and Tobago you must check with immigration. An arriving crew member needs to arrive with a letter signed by the captain stating he or she is part of the crew. If you are in Trinidad, one of the marina offices can help produce an approved letter.

Storing a Yacht

If you are leaving your yacht in storage, you need to check with the yard who is looking after it, and get them to supply you with the necessary paperwork, which is quite routine. You then take this to be stamped and approved by a customs officer in Chaguaramas.

When returning to Trinidad have these papers handy along with a list of any boat parts you are bringing in. This allows the captain (and only the captain) to transfer these items to the Chaguaramas customs station for proper duty-free entry on to your yacht. Whether you have parts or not, when you arrive back into Trinidad you must report to the Chaguaramas immigration within 24 hours.

Shipping in parts

Parts arriving from overseas via courier

will go to the Chaguaramas customs office. You will need your boat papers to get them released.

Note that while yacht parts are duty free, other items including power tools, food and household items will be charged duty.

Pets

While Trinidad does have rabies in their bat population it has not reached their small land animal population. To keep it this way they have strict regulations with regard to pets. Pets must be kept on board at all times, even when a boat is on dry land. If a pet gets sick, you can get a vet to visit the boat. It is illegal to walk the pet ashore under any circumstances. If you have a pet on board and wish to leave with it by plane (or vice versa) this must be arranged in advance. First you need an in transit permit from the Vetinary services division (phone 622-1221) then you need to arrange a quarantine guard (phone 622-5986).

There may be some changes in these laws to make it easier for pet owning yachtspeople in the next year or two.

VHF RADIO

Trinidad is part of the International Telecommunications Union. The VHF is designated specifically for safety and essential communications between vessels. Yacht users are requested to keep their transmissions brief and to use low power where possible. The VHF is not the right medium for exchanging recipes, opinions and post mortems of last nights bridge game. However, if messages are brief no one minds people using the radio to arrange a rendez-vous.

Please note that the general use channels are: 1, 4, 5, 7, 8, 9, 18, 21, 22, 23, 61, 62, 63, 65, 66, 71, 77, 80, 81, 82, 83, and 88. No other channel should be used for general communication including 68. Yachts sometimes use 68 as a calling frequency which is fine, but it should be noted that it is also a valid working channel for commercial vessels, so will sometimes be busy.

If you are calling a yard, then Peaks is on 69, Power Boats on 72, TTYA, TTYC, CrewsInn and IMS are on 68.

There is an unofficial radio net on VHF channel 68 at 0800. This shares information among yachts about weather, safety and cultural events.

PROTECTING THE ENVIRONMENT

Anchoring

Probably the worst damage yachts do to the environment is to coral when anchoring. Always anchor in sand or mud. If you have to anchor in an area with a lot of coral, dive on your anchor to make sure it is not doing any harm. If necessary, use two anchors to stop your rode from chewing up the bottom as the boat swings around.

Garbage

Take your garbage to a proper facility. Never throw anything over the side, and never discharge oil or oily bilge water while in Trinidad and Tobago waters.

SAILING EVENTS AND REGATTAS

Trinidad's keen boating community puts on some great races and competitions. Visiting yachts are encouraged to join in.

For details contact the Trinidad and Tobago Yachting Association at 634-4376.

Angostura/Yachting World Regatta

The premier event is the Angostura/Yachting World Regatta in Tobago which lasts a week and begins around the middle of May. This is one time of year you do not have to go to Scarborough to clear in. For a week preceding the race yachts coming from abroad can clear in at Store Bay. There are races for racing, cruising, charter and live-aboard classes. The regatta is big enough to be bustling and fun, yet small enough to be friendly and personal. The regatta kicks off with two days of racing followed by the best Caribbean lay day, then finishes with two more race days. There is plenty of partying and fun after the races, including volleyball competitions, treasure hunts and spontaneous jump-ups.

Trinidad and Tobago Match Racing Regatta

Teams of three compete in 20 ft SR Max sports sloops which are provided by the Yachting Association. It is held late may or early June - apply in plenty of time. A dinner party with live music is held on the night of the skipper's briefing.

The Great Race to Tobago

You will need quite a tender to compete in this, Trinidad's premier Power boat race. It is held on the first Saturday in July, and the entrants are impressive. The record for the 86 mile open-water course is just 1 hour 4 minutes.

Bum Boat Regatta

For most yachtspeople this will be a spectator event as small open sailing workboats from Tobago and islands as far north as St. Vincent compete in a series of races. Usually at Whitsuntide.

Annual Sports Fishing Competitions

The Trinidad and Tobago Game Fishing Association (T:624-5304) holds four annual events. The largest is the Carib International Game Fishing Tournament in the second half of April. Other tournaments are in the second half of March, second half of June and second half of November

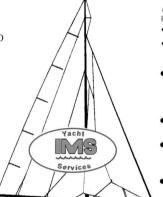

HAULED OUT AT PEAKE

YSATT

A few years ago there was no yachting industry in Trinidad. Today it is the major haul out, repair and storage destination in the Caribbean. This meteoric growth owes much to the determination and dedication of those working in this area. They realized from the outset that yachts were fickle customers, and that a careless attitude, sloppy work or over-pricing would quickly drive the yachts away.

I know of no other place in the Caribbean where such an effort is made to try and keep people happy. Part of this is done through the Yacht Service Association of Trinidad and Tobago otherwise known as YSATT. YSATT represents an ever increasing number of businesses working with the yachts.

Their offices are in the Power Boats complex, upstairs in the contractors building (YSATT c\o PBMFL, P.O.Box 3163, Carenage, Trinidad, West Indies. T: 634 4938). Their goal is to promote and enhance the proper development of this industry, and if you find things run well or if you run into problems you should drop by and talk to Ann Farfan. She will listen carefully to your recommendations and if you have a real problem she will try to help sort it out.

TIDCO

Tidco is a company that works for the government to encourage and monitor the growth of industry including yachting. If you need information before you come to Trinidad you can call Tidco's yachting rep-

resentative, Katrina Kelshall. If you are in the USA call 1-800-595-1868, from the UK call: 0 500-89-2313, from Germany call: 0 130 81 16 18 or from Italy call: 1678 70272. In Trinidad 624-2953/0234. Tidco maintains a Marine page on the internet at http://www.tidco.co.tt/local/marine.

How to haul and keep smiling

This is an industry that started with very little and had to hoist itself up on the skill and adaptability of many workers who had little experience with yachts. They have done a tremendous job, but naturally there have been a few problems and mistakes. In talking to people who have hauled here (as I do myself) it was apparent that those of us who had a lot of experience in the Caribbean were highly satisfied with the kind of service we got. Most complaints came from people who expected everything to run as smoothly and on schedule as in the USA. If you are going to haul and keep smiling, it is as well to understand the process and the people a little.

Trinidadian's love to please and they generally have an optimistic outlook. This makes them pleasant to deal with, but it can also lead to promises of delivery dates which can only be met under the most ideal conditions and these rarely prevail. This is particularly so if you pressure a contractor and plead with him to be able to do a job sooner than he feels he can. He wants to oblige so he will end up offering to try.

The weather plays a big role in any outside work. Rain is frequent and often unpredictable. Sometimes a small shower will fall on what seems like a clear blue day - It may be light, but it takes very little to destroy a paint job. Those that have serious deadlines for painting should opt to have the boat painted under cover which can be done either at Peake or CrewsInn.

Problems also arise with people who want a gold-plate job at rock bottom prices. Trinidad offers a large variety of skill levels and prices. There are many who can produce a reasonable workmanlike job at a fair price. There are a few who can do a superb job and their price is higher. If you ask around and get good recommendations you will find you can get what you need at the level you need it. In general price bargaining is not part of the local culture, and problems can occur when people try to bargain the price down to an unreasonable level. The contractor, with his sunny disposition, may want the job and agree to a lower price. But having done this, it is not going to be his top priority job nor is he going to put his best men on it.

How the yards work

Yards vary according to how much work they do themselves and how much is passed onto outside contractors. Power Boats is at one end of this continuum. They just haul and chock your boat. After that you discuss what you want done with them and they will put you in touch with a variety of contractors. These contractors are very carefully vetted. Power Boats takes a commission from the contractors which increases the price a little, but is money well spent, for the contract is signed in the Power Boats office and they stand by the work. This means that if you have a problem, you don't have to chase after some elusive contractor, you can go right into Power Boats office to get it sorted out. It also means they do their best to make sure you get your job done on time, which is a big help if you leave your boat and fly home.

CrewsInn which was just getting going as we went to press, were planning to be just the opposite. They were planning to have all their own workers, be responsible for their own work, and not allow in outside contractors. The other yards lie between these two. They have some of their own workers and they bring in outside contractors when they cannot do the job themselves.

With the exception of CrewsInn you can haul the boat and do the work yourself and

CHAGUARAMAS ANCHORAGE

25

you can hire dayworkers to help you. This works very well for people who are used to working this way. If you want a particular contractor you can also arrange this with the yard.

Preparations for yacht storage

While you are gone your yacht is going to be subject to the ravages of sun and rain. Careful preparation can do much to make your return more pleasant.

The biggest danger from rain is that your boat will fill up with water from mast and other leaks leading to flood damage. It is best to remove a hose from one of your lower seacocks and leave it open, so water entering the hull can flow out again. In addition pay someone reliable to pump your bilge from time to time, and to check your cockpit drains do not get filled with leaves.

On the inside of your boat the damp of the rainy season can play havoc with mold and condensation. This depends on how well your yacht is insulated. If it is prone to condensation then it is probably worth renting a de-humidifier to keep it dry. These are generally in short supply, so it is worth booking one well in advance.

Sun shining through windows can fade fabrics and a combination of heat and direct sunlight will destroy the display on electronic instruments. If possible remove your electronic diplays and store them below. If this is not possible, then cover them well from all direct sun. If you have large windows, then curtain them with some cheap fabric to protect the interior of the boat against the sun. If you have windows or hatches made of lexan (perspex) these too will last longer if protected, as the sun can also cause them to be covered in tiny cracks.

Electrics

You need to decide how you want to leave your electrics (connected or disconnected), If connected, it is well worth cleaning and putting some protective coating on all major terminals before you leave. You can arrange with the yard to put a charger on your batteries from time to time.

Engines

Many people do just walk away from their engines and find they work fine when they get back. However, it is worth the work of doing at least a minimum lay-up. Your fuel tank wants to be full to cut down on condensation. The salt water should be drained from the cooling system and flushed out with fresh. The engine oil should be changed. Any airways into the engine should be sealed off. This means the exhaust and the air intake. These can usually be stopped up with plastic bags.

Before stowing your outboard, run the fuel tank dry, remove the spark plug and spray a little light oil in the cylinder. Replace the spark plug lightly.

Before you leave there are some simple customs formalities that need to be dealt with. See our Customs section for details.

WELCOME TO OUR OUTHAUL AND STORAGE FACILITY AT CHAGUARAMAS BAY, TRINIDAD.

VERY ATTRACTIVE RATES ON WORK AND STORAGE

THE ON-SITE FACILITIES
- 50 ton marine hoist
- Telephone and fax services
- Free water and electricity
- Mast removal
- Refueling dock - gasoline & diesel
- Laundramat, toilets & showers
- Snackbar & grocery
- Woodwork, upholstery & electrical shops
- Sale repair loft & marine store
- Space on land for 160 boats
- Stern-to dock space for 22 boats
- Self contained apartments for rent
- Stockists of AB dinghies

THE WORK:
- Skilled and semi-skilled labour for sanding, painting, welding, woodworking, engine repairs, fiberglassing
- Sail and rigging repairs
- Very comprehensive machine shop work for propeller repairs and all aluminum, stainless steel and bronze repairs
- Osmosis repairs using state-of-the-art peeling machinery & drying methods
- Bona fide crews are allowed to work on their boats free of charge.
- Gelcoat restoration.

AND REMEMBER:
- Trinidad is out of the main hurricane belt
- Teak is grown in Trinidad and is readily available at excellent prices

Power Boat Mutual Facilities Ltd.,
P.O. Box 3163, Carenage, Trinidad, W. I.
Tel: (809) 634•4303 Fax: (809) 634•4327.
E-mail: pbmfl@trinidad.net
VHF: Ch. 72 call "PowerBoats".

Power Boats

RED HOWLER MONKEY, ROGER NECKLES PHOTO

It would be a crime to spend time in Trinidad without doing some sightseeing. There are few places in the world where so many beautiful birds and animals exist in such a small area. There is also beautiful scenery and some dramatic waterfalls. It is easiest to rent a car or make arrangements with a tour operator or taxi, but some sightseeing can be done by bus.

Caroni Swamp

One of the most famous destinations is the Caroni Swamp, where you can see Trinidad and Tobago's national bird, the scarlet ibis. These sociable birds congregate at night on small mangrove islands which can only be approached by boat. The only practical way to see them is to join an organized tour. It is best to call in advance, but you can just turn up at the Caroni Swamp car park after 1500 and make arrangements on the spot. Take the road south from Port of Spain toward San Fernando and look for the turn off to the Caroni Swamp which is clearly signposted. Bring binoculars, bug spray and a sun hat or visor and sunglasses, as the sun can be glaring for the first half hour.

You will be taken by boat through a maze of mangrove channels which are home to herons, mangrove crabs and oddities like the four-eyed fish. The climax of the trip, however is seeing the scarlet ibis. The beauty of this gorgeous red bird, luminous in the late afternoon sun, is beyond description. The lowest level of the mangrove island fills with snowy egrets and little blue herons occupy the mid-level. Then the ibises arrive in small groups from their feeding grounds, gliding gracefully to roost until hundreds of them stand out like brilliant flowers against a dark green background. Winston Nanan's tours are led by knowledgeable guides.

The ibis show is at twilight and an earlier stop at Chaguanas, just a few miles farther south, provides an appealing contrast. This town, dominated by East Indians, is a thriving commercial center and an inexpensive place to shop. Wander up and down the colorful main road where end-to-end street vendors have their goods on display.

Asa Wright Nature Center

This 200-acre nature preserve is set in gorgeous mountain scenery at an elevation of about 1200 feet. To get there you take the eastern main road to Arima and then head north.

The nature center was formerly part of a cocoa, coffee and citrus plantation. In 1950

William Beebe established a tropical research station nearby and visiting scientists often stayed at the Wright's. One of these, Don Eckelberry, a renown bird painter, persuaded Asa Wright to turn her property into a reserve after the death of her husband.

It is easy to sit for hours on the verandah of the beautiful old estate house, built in 1907, and watch the birds come to you. Well stocked feeders bring hummingbirds, honey creepers, woodpeckers and many other birds right up close.

The estate has daily tours with local naturalists who will point out many birds you would otherwise miss. You can also hike on any of the marked trails. A day here may not seem enough and they do have overnight accommodation, usually used by birding enthusiasts from the USA. You need to book in advance for lunch and this you should do as it is miles from anywhere. There is a reasonable admission charge.

Allow time to return by the northern route which follows miles of breathtaking mountain and cliff top scenery.

Timberline

Timberline Resort and Nature Center at Pointe Vache makes an excellent lunch stop when you are touring the north coast. Do not be intimidated by the road which does a fair imitation of a ski slope. It is not quite as terrifying as it looks, and all but the most wimpy car will make the return trip up the hill. Timberline is set in an old estate and mill which are built on a ridge with views in both directions. On a clear day you can see both Tobago and Venezuela. Beneath is one of the best north coast anchorages. Timberline is always open for lunch on weekends and holidays and also on most weekdays. At other times it is essential to call in advance or you may find the whole place locked up.

The Pitch Lake

This pond of asphalt was described by Noel Coward as "22 tennis courts badly in need of repair," but perhaps he had some oversize courts in mind for this million-year old pit covers 89 acres. Sir Walter Raleigh was the first European to describe it and he used the pitch as caulking compound for his

VIOLACEOUS TROGON, ROGER NECKLES PHOTO

fleet. The quality of the asphalt is high and approximately 300 tons a day are removed. The pitch lake is about 10 miles southeast of San Fernando, near the small town of Brighton.

Maracas Waterfall

The Maracas Waterfall is 300 feet high, the highest in the country. Compared with some other waterfalls in the Caribbean it is not particularly dramatic but the drive into the mountains and the 1.5 mile hike up to the falls is pleasant through lovely country. There is a good picnicking area at the falls.

Fort George

When the crowds, bustle or daily routine start to annoy, drive the five minutes from the yacht club up to Fort George (open 0600 to 1800). It is a whole different world up here, a peaceful spot with spectacular views over Port of Spain. You can also see all the way over to North Post. Fort George was built to defend Trinidad in 1805. It was converted to a signal station in 1902 and was used as late as 1964. The views and the well tended gardens make it a peaceful place to relax. You often see parrots.

Turtle Watch Tours

Everyone I met who went turtle watching, was delighted. Seeing one of these giant sea reptiles emerge from the sea, their shells glistening in the moon, to struggle up the sand and lay their eggs, a behavior evolved millions of years ago, is enthralling. Trinidad is the best place in the Eastern Caribbean to experience this. Leatherback turtles are most commonly seen. They are six to seven feet long and weigh up to a ton. The eggs take 60 days to hatch. From March to June as many as 30 to 60 turtles may arrive on some beaches in one night. Some nesting continues until September. While the volume of nesting turtles decreases after June, the chances of seeing young hatching out increases. Turtles nest on the northeast and east coast. Matura Bay is a popular and accessible site which is closely controlled and well run. There is a small government fee to pay. One of the nicest places for a turtle watch is at Grande Riviere on Trinidad's north coast. This is because there is a charming small hotel on the beach called Mt. Plasir Estate (C). It is run by Piero Guerrini from Italy and makes a perfect dinner spot and base for a watch. They have several communal rooms with up to 6 beds for groups. The only disadvantage is the drive from Chaguaramas, which takes three to four hours.

There are many excellent hikes and waterfalls in the Grande Riviere area, so any extra time you can arrange to spend (even half a day) will be well rewarded. Hiking can be arranged through the hotel.

Avoid public holidays if possible as this often increases the crowd considerably. The beach and the turtles appear more beautiful when the moon is close to full. On the other hand the full moon may also bring more people. If there is a crowd, consider eating dinner and sleeping till 0130, by which time most people will have left. Take plenty of bug spray. I enjoyed having a small beach seat for relaxed viewing. Heavy rain may also affect landings. The easiest way to turtle watch is join a tour or rent a car.

33

TREE PORCUPINE, ROGER NECKLES PHOTO

Nariva Swamp

I am standing precariously balanced on a tree trunk that spans a narrow mangrove lined waterway. I am clutching my camera and binoculars in one had and holding onto a branch with the other. Roger Neckles, my guide, stands beside me nursing his even more expensive camera gear. Charmou, our boatman has our ten foot boat half under part of the tree and he tugs and cutlasses at the obstruction that blocks our path. This is the Nariva swamp and it is well off the beaten track. The Nariva swamp lies on the east coast about half-way down Trinidad. It is one of the richest wildlife areas in the country. From our small dinghy we look out over a large expanse of grassy swampland with many areas of tall royal palms. We see and hear parrots all around. Suddenly Roger hears a different sound and points - a pair of red bellied macaws fly among the trees, their brilliant colors easy to see through binoculars. It is the first of several sightings we will make as we continue up the creek. Every now and again our boatman stops and puts his hand in the water to bring up a conk - a large freshwater snail I am assured is delicious. Birdlife along the bank is good: we see anis, kites, white headed marsh tyrants and pied water tyrants. Several types of hawk stand silhouetted on the top of dead tree stumps. Our destination is Bushbush

Island in the middle of the swamp. Here we apply liberal amounts of bug spray and head down a small trail. We are looking for the white capuchin monkey. Roger looks around and says - "I think they are watching us, they are very crafty." Roger does his imitation of a white capuchin monkey and is rewarded by a distant cry. We are off at high speed in the direction of the sound through the bush, trying to avoid the more prickly plants.

We arrive in the general area and Roger calls again. Nothing. While scanning the trees we hit on another delightful find - the channel-billed toucan, high in a tree above us, a perfect view. Monkey sounds come again in a different direction and once more we are rushing through the bush, this time to be rewarded by the site of two monkeys climbing through the trees above.

Roger explains that the capuchin monkeys are often found near red howler monkeys. The red howler monkey is larger and more fierce but slower. He also has a better sense of smell. So when the red howler goes hunting the capuchin monkeys follow. As the howler monkeys get close to the tree in fruit, the capuchin monkeys pick up the scent. They shoot past the howler monkeys and get to the fruit first, eating as much as they can before howler monkeys catch up and chase them away.

We are hoping to catch sight of the red howler monkeys and go to an area Roger often finds them. There is nothing but the distant sound of a troup far away. We give up and head back. About halfway down the trail we hear the howler monkeys - a blood-curdling sound, a throaty angry roaring noise, like a bunch of angry lions and bears hell bent on destruction. We are off running through the bush again, far from silently, but the monkeys are making so much noise they don't hear us till we approach, by which time they decide the best way to get rid of us is to scare us with a magnificent display of noise. Their throats looking enormous as they cry.

It has been a lucky day. Roger says he often sees the monkeys but not always. Our luck continues on the way back when we see the rare white tailed gold throated hummingbird and a Venezuelan fly catcher.

Lakes

Trinidad has three large water storage dams; Hollis Reservoir, Nevit Dam and Arena Dam. These are all excellent areas for hiking and picnicking, a wonderful way to get away from the boat for a day. They are off the main roads so it is probably best to rent a car. You can expect to see a good collection of water birds including cormorants and ducks. You might even get to see caimans.

I have only been to Arena, the largest of these. Here they have built facilities including shelters and tables. It covers a large area so should there be a crowd, you will be able to get well away. Unfortunately trees do not come all the way down to the water which is sided by a large area of grass, but it is still an attractive place. You may be able to canoe on Arena dam, and I would think that includes a rubber dinghy if that is what you have. Take oars or paddles because outboards are not allowed, and get permission from WASA before you go. You do need a pass from WASA to visit these dams, and there is a moderate fee to pay. You can call WASA for details at: 662-2301/5, 622-1965.

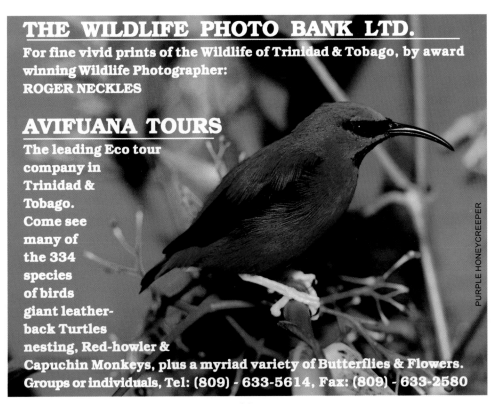
35

WHERE TO GO FOR TOURS:

Avifauna Tours, contact Roger Neckles Tel: 633-5614. Roger Neckles is Trinidad's leading wildlife photographer, an excellent birder and naturalist. A tour with Roger is particularly recommended for small groups serious about either photography or nature. The more exotic wildlife is often best observed early in the morning, so he may suggest starting as early as 0530. Roger also knows some special locations in the northern range, unknown to other operators. He will also go with just one person.

Sail and Fly at Peake, contact Michael Bauza, Tel: 634-4144, VHF:68. Sail and Fly organize a variety of tours with yachtspeople in mind. These are tours where you join a group of others (usually about 8). Their turtle watch tours which go to Grande Riviere have been particularly successful and are recommended.

Kayak Tours, contact Mr. Meryl See Tai, Tel: 629-2680. A variety of Kayaking tours are available through Mr. Meryl See Tai. These are adventure type trips in areas of great beauty, but keep in mind that kayaks are not always the best place to take expensive camera gear. The main areas they cover are; The Nariva Swamp including Bush-Bush sanctuary, The Caroni swamp and the Oropuche River near San Fernando.

TRINIDAD CARNIVAL

by Cathy Winn

DENYSE PLUMMER, QUEEN OF CALYPSO

It's called the greatest show on earth; it's a riotous display of color and music; it's a national three day festival which showcases the boundless imagination, creativity and love of life that Trinidadians share with the rest of the world at this time of the year. If you can plan your stay to include Carnival try to do so; it will truly amaze you and prove to be one of the highlights of your Caribbean travels.

Trinidad's Carnival is unique in that it is a truly democratic festival; everyone can and does participate. It is not an event where you have to stand behind a barrier and take pictures although you can if you wish. But the thrill of Carnival is to participate; get muddy in your old clothes along with everyone else on J'Ouvert morning, buy a sexy bright feathered costume and strut your stuff on Tuesday. Cruisers can and have done all this and still have plenty of great pictures to shock their grandchildren with. Carnival is what you make of it and there is indeed something for every taste.

Many of the traditions of Trinidad Carnival originated in medieval Europe and West Africa brought by early immigrants from the former, and their slaves from the latter. The many different peoples and different classes created their quite different carnivals, illustrating the attempt to come to terms with each other. "French Creole" Carnival was exclusive, a culmination of a long Christmas season. It was a time of fancy dress balls, a diversion giving some excitement to their lives. Oddly enough these whites had a favorite "masque" of imitating their Negro slaves and reenacted activities on the cane plantations with torches to portray cane fires. This "canboulay" was a traditional part of the festivities on the plantations.

The Negroes were allowed a certain freedom during these times and began to have their own costuming, often mimicking their masters ways and dress. Emancipation occurring in 1833, resulting in a withdrawal of the Creoles from much of the public festivities but a renewed exuberance from the freed slaves. Gradually the activities became very rowdy with glorification of the "jammette" class, or the underworld. There were stick fighting, devil characters, midnight robbers, and flagrant sexual parody, mimicking the ways of life of a deviant working class. Attempts were made to limit and even outlaw Carnival, but were always bitterly fought by mobs and even middle class black nationalists. Over regulation is still resisted today sternly by Trinidadians who insist on having Carnival their way. Gradually as the Carnival became more law-abiding, the middle

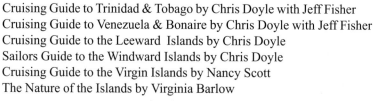

ALYSON BROWN, CARNIVAL QUEEN 1995

class, and "French Creoles" began to come out in the streets again. Competitions sponsored by early merchants were started for best costume and Carnival became more respectable while still retaining a working class rearguard which is still active today in J'Ouvert. There is growing interest today in reviving and keeping alive some of the old ways, and for years now yachties have been thrilled by the Ole Time Carnival parade and show, with many of the characters being portrayed without the lawlessness of previous years.

When to come, what to do

While Carnival proper is just the three days and nights before Ash Wednesday, the buildup starts just after Christmas and makes up a whole season of events and parties (or fetes as they as called), as well as Panorama, the steel band competitions. You will be doing yourself a disservice if you arrive only the week of Carnival; many of the best parties will be over, the anchorages will be very crowded and tickets and costumes almost impossible to get. Give yourself time to explore, feel comfortable and choose how you want to enjoy this time. There is so much to do and see that you can easily be overwhelmed. Jack Dausend, of the yacht Wind Psalm, a veteran of six Carnivals here, gives "don't miss" seminars to help you make sense of the vocabulary and schedule, and to help you make the best choices of what to see and take part in. At these seminars you can find out dates of events, how the transportation is arranged, how to be safe on the streets, find out what other cruisers are doing for Carnival, and be entertained as well. These semi-nars are generally held once a week starting about six weeks before Carnival.

Even before Christmas, most of the Carnival costume makers have set up their "camps" with pictures of their costumes which revolve around a central theme chosen by each camp leader. It is essential to go around to these "mas camps" (mas is short for masquerade) and preview each leader's attempt to win the coveted "Band of the Year" title. Tours of the mas camps are arranged from all the anchoring areas so you can see many of them in one evening. These camps are where everyone signs up for and receives their costumes, so a tour is a good chance to view the field before making your final decision. And if one really takes your fancy you can volunteer to help make costumes for a day.

KING OF CARNIVAL, 1993

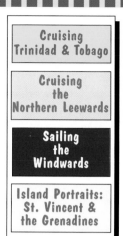
The weeks before Carnival are also the time of year for the island-wide steel band festival and competition called Panorama which comes to a grand finale the weekend before Carnival. All of Trinidad converges on the Savannah to support their favorite group and to see all their friends who come home to Trinidad every year for Carnival. The one hundred member-strong groups play original compositions written new every season, some composed especially for them. The competitions go into the wee hours of the morning, to give each band a chance at the title. Go with a group to visit the "pan yards" and hear them practice before the competitions, you can really get up close. You can even join a steelband, as every year, at least one yachtie does and tries to master this instrument.

Fetes and more fetes

During the Carnival season everyone goes to fetes, held at many places all over Port of Spain and environs. Here all the new music for the season can be heard, everyone shows off their cool clothes, there's lots of great food, drinking, dancing and flirting. Dancing is easy to this music; you don't need a partner. Just move as the music moves you, and it certainly will. Ear plugs are recommended for neophytes because high volume is de-rigeur at fetes. By the time Carnival comes around you'll probably already have a favorite "soca" tune and know several calypsos too. Soca is the danceable music you'll hear on the road while calypso is the more traditional music with a message you'll hear in "tents" at various venues throughout town. Don't miss these Calypso nights at the tents. Trinidad is the home of this particular kind of song and they'll truly give you a good idea of Trini style. Fetes are open to the public; tickets are necessary and the really popular ones are sold out way in advance. Some of the best are charity events and for one all-inclusive price you can eat, drink, and party to a live band and a DJ for hours.

Getting around

So you may be wondering how you're going to get to all these great events from

41

the Chaguaramas anchorages? Rest assured, the yachting community in Trinidad has successfully moved hundreds of boaters to all the events via buses and maxi-taxis. There are sign-up sheets at each marina and for a nominal fee you are assured of safe reliable transport to almost all the big events during Carnival. Names and numbers of proven reliable "maxis" are provided so you and your friends can also set up your own trips. Bulletin boards are made available at the marinas so you can be kept up to date on what's coming up.

Calender of events

Let me give you a brief calendar of events which make up Carnival. Dimanche Gras (French for big Sunday) is a formal show requiring advance tickets. At this show you will see the finalists for the King and Queen of Carnival, the Calypso Monarch competition interspersed with dance routines from several local companies. Traditionally it is a very long show, almost five hours, and the winners are announced at the end. It is now early Monday morning which officially signals the start of Carnival at 2 a.m. with J'Ouvert (French for daybreak).

J'Ouvert is known for the mud, oil, and grease that many masqueraders spread all over themselves. Steelbands also take to the streets with their fans and it is bacchanal time all over Port of Spain until nine a.m. or so. Then, after a bath and a short rest and meal, those hearty revelers come out again to play "mas" in the streets, this time in their fancy pretty costume but not in the full regalia you will see on Tuesday. Monday night mas is very popular; most groups have a low-key costume, maybe just a T-shirt and funny hat.

Tuesday the action starts early; the first band is on the stage of the Savannah by eight a.m. in their full costume and continues on all day. Around seven p.m., at the Harvard Roundabout, there is a steelband competition called Las Lap for those who still aren't tired. At midnight Tuesday Carnival is officially over and all music stops. Lent now begins and Trinidadians flock to churches and the beaches on Ash Wednesday, to wash away their Carnival sins. And you, sleeping in late for once back at your boat, can look back at Trinidad Carnival and have wonderful memories to take back home with you.

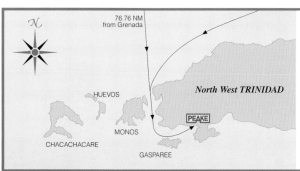

Trinidad from Grenada

It is 78 miles from Prickly Bay to the north coast of Trinidad. Most people leave Prickly Bay around dusk and sail overnight. The light on Chacachacare is excellent and helps confirm your position. The tidal stream between Grenada and Trinidad is patchy so if you use a GPS to stay on course you will be upwind one minute and falling off the next. Better make an average estimate for current. On the return trip to Grenada remember that the current can be strongest close to Grenada.

The most usual and direct entrance into the Gulf of Paria is through the Boca de Monos. There is a small island about a third of the way between Monos Island and the mainland. Pass between this island and the mainland. There are shoals and rocks between this island and Monos Island.

Trinidad from Venezuela

If wind and sea are against you from the eastern tip of Venezuela, you will probably find it easier to pass on the south side of Chacachacare and the other islands, where you will be out of the ocean swells.

Tobago from Trinidad

Sailing from Trinidad to Tobago is tough because you are bucking both wind and current. It is only about 60 miles from Scotland Bay but it seems longer. The conventional approach is to power up the Trinidad coast at night when the wind is generally lighter, and cross over to Tobago early in the morning. It makes the crossing shorter and more pleasant to set off early in the morning and stop at a north coast anchorage. (See our North Coast Anchorage Section.) If you leave a north coast anchorage about midnight and power up the coast, you should arrive at Galera Point early the next morning. Don't forget to string out the fishing line during daylight hours to pick up your next meal.

The north coast of Trinidad is mainly steep to, but it is difficult to gauge distances at night so I would stay about a mile offshore. Close to shore you sometimes get a counter current which normally goes east at the beginning of the rising tide for about four hours. This can be a mixed blessing when the wind is blowing hard as it creates nasty short seas.

Some experienced Trinidad yachtsmen manage to find a counter current a little way off Trinidad's north coast. They motor sail, staying in the current until it dies out and then strike out for Tobago.

When you reach Galera Point you will find a current of at least two-knots sweeping westward between Trinidad and Tobago. Even if you sail hard on the wind, heading to the east end of Tobago, you will be lucky to make it close to Crown Point (watch out for the shoals). From Crown Point it is a tough three-hour motor sail to Scarborough. If you want to go to Scarborough, it is easiest to motor sail from Galera Point to make it in one tack.

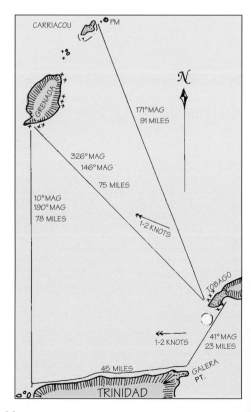

Tobago from Grenada

The cruising yachtsperson with plenty of time who wants to visit both Trinidad and Tobago might consider visiting Tobago first, setting off from Grenada's sister Island Carriacou. If you leave in the afternoon and sail round to the northeast side of Carriacou and pass between Carriacou and PSV (there are shoals so you should not do it too late in the afternoon) you get an excellent shot at making Tobago in one tack. When you arrive in Tobago you will still have to make the struggle up wind to Scarborough to clear in.

People also sail from Grenada to Tobago. The speed of this passage varies with the wind direction and current. Most people leave at dusk and go overnight. If you need to tack, don't do it close to Grenada where the current is strongest. If you have a GPS you can gauge when you are out of the current.

TRINIDAD

Regulations

Customs regulations are simple and straightforward.

Go straight to the customs dock in Chaguaramas with your yacht on arrival. Those arriving or leaving out of normal weekday office hours (0800-1200 and 1300-1600) will be charged overtime (around $45 US). Customs stand by on VHF:16. See also the details given in our Cruising Information chapter.

Holidays

January 1 - New Year's Day
Carnival - the Monday and Tuesday 40 days before Easter are not official holidays - but just try to do anything but fete!
Easter Friday through Monday
Whit Monday (7 weeks after Easter)
Corpus Christi (Thursday, 12 days after Whit Sunday)
19th June - Labor Day
1st August - Emancipation Day
31st August - Independence Day
24th September - Republic Day
25th December - Christmas Day
26th December - Boxing Day
Moveable holidays include Eid (Muslim - April) and Divali (Hindu - October, November)
If you cannot figure out when easter is, pick up a copy of the annual "Boater's Directory" which gives all the annual holiday dates.

Shopping hours

Shopping hours are normally 0800-1200 and 1300-1630. Most shops close Saturday afternoons and not much happens on a Sunday. Shopping malls often do not open till 0900 or 0930 but they usually stay open until at least 2200 and many open Sunday mornings. Most banks open 0800 to 1400 Monday to Thursday and on Fridays from 0800 to 1200 and 1500 to 1800.

Telephones

Trinidad has public card phones dotted all over the country. You can buy cards at all marinas and clubs. In Port of Spain you can get them at the main Telecommunications Services Trinidad and Tobago (TSTT) in the Maritime Life building on the south side of Independence square at Edward Street.

For USA, Canada and other Caribbean islands with a three digit code, dial 1+ the 10 digit number. For other overseas calls dial 01 + the country code + the number.

Card phones cannot currently be used for credit card or collect calls.

(continued)

47

There are USA direct lines at most yacht service facilities. There is also a USA direct line at TSTT.

For incoming calls Trinidad is like a USA number with an area code of 809. This area code will change to 868 in June 1997.

Currency

The currency is the Trinidad and Tobago (TT) dollar which floats with other currencies. At last count it was about $5.8TT to $1US.

Transport

Trinidad is well served by major airlines and has a large international airport. It also has its own airline, BWIA, whose schedule is sometimes more convenient than the other carriers. There is a $75TT departure tax, which you can avoid if you are leaving directly from a yacht.

Locals who do not have cars in Trinidad usually travel by maxi taxis which are the cheapest way to get around. These are minibuses that work certain routes and cover most of Trinidad. Like regular taxis they have "H" number plates. Find a bus stop on the road in the direction you want to go and stick your hand out. (This last action is absolutely necessary or they do not stop.) Ask the driver if he or she is going in your direction. They will sometime go out of the way for a small fee. If the taxi you stop has no other passengers on board, confirm with the driver that it is a maxi taxi and not a private taxi. If you are leaving from Port of Spain, join the maxi taxi at the starting point, as they always leave full.

Rental cars are available (check our directory). US, Canadian, UK and most European residents can drive up to three months on their own licenses. International licences are also accepted. Drive on the Left.

Private Taxis are plentiful. Sample rates (which may well rise) are:

	$TT
All day tours	300
Power Boats to town	35
Yacht Club to town	35
TTYA to airport	150
Power Boats to St. James	30
Power Boats to Caroni Swamp*	200
By the hour	40

*(round trip, does not include the boat)

Local Radio:

610 or 730 AM, 91,95, 97, 100, 105 or 106 FM.

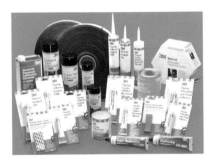

TRINIDAD

SIE '93

They say that when Columbus discovered Trinidad he stumbled into a big party. Today, Trinidadians are fun loving, hospitable people who do indeed love partying. Steel pan music was invented here, a by product of the oil industry and all the discarded oil drums. Calypso, too, had its birth in Trinidad. These musical forms combine to help make Trinidad's carnival the world's finest celebration.

Trinidad seems to reach out and almost touch Venezuela. The two were linked together only 11,000 years ago when the last ice age lowered the sea by 300 feet. It shares a rich diversity of plants, birds and insects with the South American continent. There are also some species which are unique to Trinidad, including the cowboy spider, a clever beast which throws its web at its prey.

When Columbus discovered himself in Trinidad in 1498, it was inhabited by South American Indians. The early Spanish colonization in 1776 was not successful as the Spanish were doing too well plundering South America to get too interested in Trinidad. Governor Chacon offered free land to all comers, and the colonization of Trinidad got under way with the help of many French settlers. Port of Spain became the main town.

The British captured Trinidad and Tobago in 1797 and held the two islands until independence. In the early days Trinidad had a flourishing plantation economy based on sugar. The plantocracy found itself short of labor after the abolition of slavery, when former slaves quite naturally wanted no part of working on the plantations. The landowners' solution to the problem was to import some 150,000 indentured servants from India. Today Trinidad's population is a blend of Indians, Africans and Europeans, a mix which has generated some exceptionally good looking people. Trinidad has a population of 1.2 million, about 350,000 of whom live in Port of Spain. Trinidad and Tobago became an independent twin-island state in 1962, a democracy in the British tradition. It has proved a stable democracy which was led by Dr. Eric Williams for 20 years until his death. Although there have been a few attempted coups over the years, none have come close to success.

During the last world war the United States established major naval and air bases in Trinidad. They served to protect oil shipments to England, which were prime targets for German U-boats. Trinidad has the good fortune to have large oil deposits and a pitch lake. As a result it is more industrialized than the rest of the Caribbean and produces, among other things, steel and ammonia. Oil

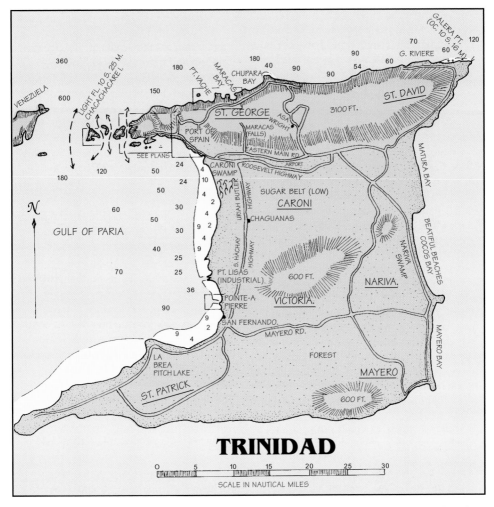

TRINIDAD

```
0        5        10       15       20       25       30
|mmmmmmmm|mmmmmmmm|mmmmmmmm|mmmmmmmm|mmmmmmmm|mmmmmmmm|
              SCALE IN NAUTICAL MILES
```

and natural gas are exported. Shipbuilding and major construction are undertaken.

Trinidad is modern. It has large shopping malls, similar to those in the USA, good roads and excellent repair facilities. Many yachts-people enjoy spending part or all of the hurricane season here. The sightseeing is good, the hospitality great, and Port of Spain is a thriving, bustling town where something is always happening. It is a great place to overhaul your boat and enjoy yourself at the same time, and a very secure place to leave your boat in dry storage.

There are a good number of Trinidadian

yachtspeople and they have two active yacht clubs, the Trinidad and Tobago Yacht Club (TTYC) and the Trinidad and Tobago Yachting Association (TTYA). They are welcoming and friendly to visiting yachtspeople and happy to see everyone having a good time.

Trinidad also has several out of the way anchorages. These make perfect getaways for a few days of peace and quiet.

CHAGUARAMAS BAY

Chaguaramas Bay is in hilly country and from the anchorage there is a pleasing view of several islands. The area supports large numbers of pelicans, corbeaus (vultures) and frigatebirds which ride the thermals like dark kites. Laughing gulls quarrel noisily over scraps of food from fishing boats. Parrots fly overhead. This anchorage is generally well protected, but when the wind comes south of east a surge comes around the corner. This lessens as you get farther in. Occasionally this surge can become dangerous, especially on the Power Boats dock which is next to the travelift dock. The water is relatively shallow here which increases the surge.

There are several yachting facilities at Chaguaramas. It is close to Monos Island, Gaspar Grande and Scotland Bay. It is within walking distance of the TTYA, access to town is easy, and many yachts use this as their base in Trinidad.

Regulations

Chaguaramas is the port of entry for visiting yachts. The officers here are friendly and clearance is straightforward. (For more details see our section on customs in Cruising Information.)

Services

In this section we describe many of the available marine services and where you will find them. Keep in mind that all the contractors we mention are not restricted to the yard where their workshop is and will work in any of the yards or on your boat.

Despite its name, Power Boats deals as much with yachts as with small power boats. They have a fuel dock with diesel, gasoline and water. It opens 0800 to 1800, except Saturday and Sunday when it opens 0600-

BOATYARDS, CHAGUARAMAS

1800. In the Power Boats office you can buy tickets for the Port of Spain bus. This runs about once every half hour and you have to have a ticket to get on. Other services include toilets and showers, a good little grocery store, launderette and rental apartments. There is room for about 22 boats to come stern-to and more docks are planned. Power Boats has a 50-ton travel lift, as well as a tractor-trailer designed specifically to haul multihulls. They can store about 200 boats on the hard. Since many yachts are left here during the hurricane season, advance booking is essential. Don Stollmeyer, the manager, is very helpful and all kinds of repairs can be arranged through a system of subcontractors. Power Boats works with these contractors and takes on the responsibility that the work is properly done. Power Boats also own a gelcoat stripper that makes easy and clean work of dealing with osmosis problems and is far preferable to sandblasting or grinding. Those anchored out are welcome to leave their dinghies behind the stern-to yacht berths. They request that you register with the office when you come ashore, and

will give you a pass to gain access through the main gate. Do not put dinghies on the power boat or stern-to docks. Power Boats is the home of several shops and sub-contractors' workshops.

The Fiberglass Specialist is a workshop close to the dinghy dock behind Shipwrights (see below). It is run by Chris Ramdhan aided by a team of about 16. He specializes in spray painting and fiberglass work and undertakes large jobs like hull extensions and solid biminis as well as smaller work of repairing, fairing and painting hulls.

There are two woodworking shops, Shipwrights is located right by the dinghy dock in a thatch roofed building and is run by Fred Thomas. Fred has been working with wooden boats since 1972 when he started his apprenticeship on the East coast of the U.S. He has owned and rebuilt 13 traditional boats since then and is the man to see for high quality workmanship. He can do anything from teak deck repairs to complete restorations and interior design and engineering, aided by the latest in computer technology.

Fortress Woodworking is located in the

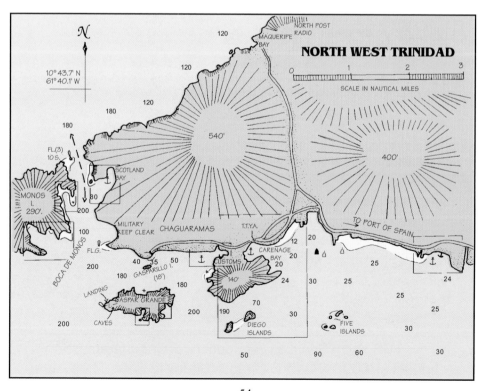

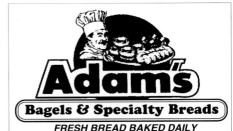

contractors' building on the east side of the compound and does all types of joinery work and has laid many a teak deck. They have a good supply of woods like teak, mahogany, purple heart and cedar as well as veneers and plywoods. One of the nicest things about this shop is that they will happily cut up pieces of wood to your specification as well as work on complete projects. Talk to Neville Boos who has his office upstairs where you can see some samples of their work.

Downstairs in the same building is The Boat Shop II (VHF 72) which has a good supply of chandlery items. They are very helpful and if you need something they do not have in stock, they will order it and have it there within a few days. Their stock includes rigging wire which they will cut to length, terminals and turnbuckles. Their other store, The Boat Shop I, in Glencoe, specializes more in power boats supplies.

Next door is Caribbean Marine (VHF 72) run by David Laughlin and their specialty is DC power and diesel injectors. They can test, diagnose, charge and sell batteries, dispose of your old ones and check out your charg-

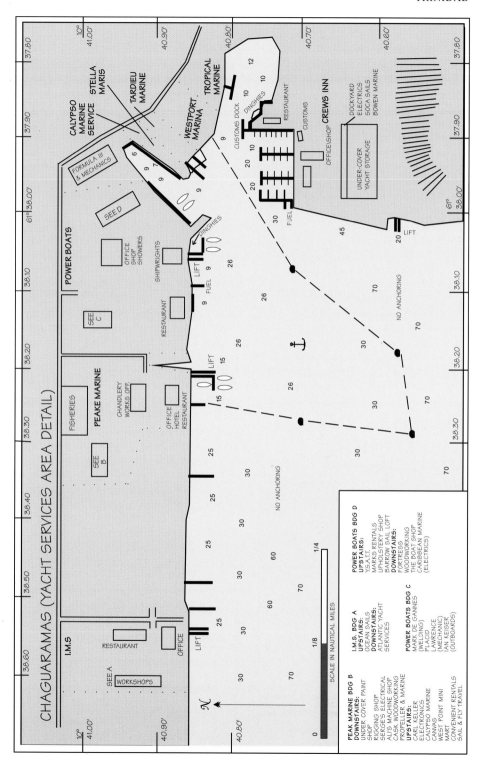

CHAGUARAMAS (YACHT SERVICES AREA DETAIL)

ing systems. They repair alternators and chargers as well as DC motors and wind generators. Solar panels are also available, as well as monitoring instruments. If you need your injectors tested he can do it on the spot.

Upstairs is the Barrow Sail Loft (VHF 68) operated by Rawl Barrow and his son. They are agents for North Sails and can do all types of repairs on sails as well as make biminis, dodgers and stainless tubing frames. They can build new sails for boats up to about 30 feet, and staysails or mizzens for larger yachts. Larger sails are ordered through North.

Next door you will find David Mahabir of The Upholstery Shop (VHF 72). He can make bunk cushions out of a variety of foam densities and fabrics. Cockpit cushions out of closed cell foam, sail covers, hatch covers or a custom cover for your inflatable to protect it from UV degradation.

Upstairs at the far end you will find the YSATT office and right next door is Mark's Rentals Limited (VHF 68) who have several types of cars for both short and long term.

They also do airport transfers and sometimes help out with taxi work.

On the west side of Power Boats, is Mark deGannes who works in aluminum and stainless steel. He can fabricate and repair tanks, pulpits, bimini and dodger frames, davits and tuna towers, using Tig, Mig or Argon welding.

In the same building, further towards the waterfront, is Ian Keizer a qualified OMC mechanic who can repair your outboard motor. Next door Placid Lawrence has a workshop and is a good general mechanic.

On the east side of Power Boats is an old hanger with two workshops and a chandlery. Stephen De Gannes and his family operate Formula III (VHF 68). They have been building power boats ranging from 12 to 40 feet for many years, as well as Legacy and C-Mos, a couple of very successful 43-foot sailing boats that have raced extensively in the area. They do all kinds of fiberglass construction and repair, including the larger and more difficult jobs. They can treat osmosis and do top grade Awlgrip painting.

In the same building is a mechanical shop shared by four mechanics, Chris De Gannes, Dessie, Colin Hamel-Smith and Robert, any of whom is happy to tackle any kind of job from outboards to diesels and generators. They can install, recondition or repair your transmission, be it an outdrive or saildrive. If you are looking for a secondhand, reconditioned power source, check them out.

This is also to be the site of a new Budget Marine chandlery. Budget Marine is the largest Caribbean chandler with stores in St. Maarten, Antigua and now Trinidad. They

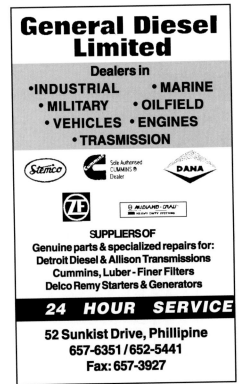

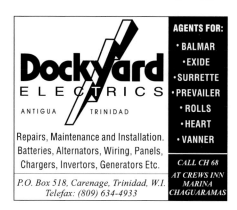
keep an excellent selection of both general and technical parts some of which are featured in their large mail-order catalogue. If they do not have it in stock you can be sure that whatever you need will be available within a day or two.

Next to Power Boats, towards the west, is Peake Yacht Services (VHF:69). They have a 150-ton travelift that can handle yachts with as much as 27.5 foot beam and 15 feet of keel below the straps. One advantage of using this lift for smaller yachts is that you do not need to remove your forestay or backstay. A 60-ton hydraulic trailer transfers the boats to the storage area and can pack them in close together to accommodate about 300 on the hard. The boats can be pressure washed as soon as they are hauled. You can work on your own boat or use the complete line of services offered by the yard. There is a special area set aside for sandblasting as well as undercover paint sheds. Their stern-to dock can accommodate about 17 boats. A small hotel called the Bight has 10 rooms and

an indoor/outdoor restaurant and bar close to the dock. Other facilities include, toilets, showers, laundry, a yacht brokerage and bike rentals. They also rent locker rooms and air conditioners if you need to stay cool. They offer a complimentary shuttle bus service to and from Port of Spain several times a day. You can tie your dinghy on the west side of the travelift dock or up on the beach next to it. The office is upstairs in the hotel building. The laundry, toilets and phones are on the other side of that same building. A Royal Bank branch is on the premises with a 24 hour teller machine.

Peake chandlery, the largest in Trinidad, is located just north of the docks. They have a truly magnificent selection of hardware including a vast range of ss screws, nuts and bolts. You will find just about everything you may need for your boat from water pumps to paint. If they don't have it in stock, they can order it for you. In the same store is a video rental for your evening's entertainment.

The services building west of the chandlery houses the undercover spray area where boats of up to 100 feet can be sprayed in a dust free environment aided by filters and ventilators. The rigging shop is also here where any kind of rigging work can be done. This is run by Bill Wray who has over 40 years experience in this field as well as being a Lloyds qualified surveyor. They are agents for Harken and Stalok, and have a swaging machine for lifelines and a cold header machine for Navtec rod rigging. They can repair winches, masts, booms, roller furling gear or have terminals X-rayed and evaluated. They can also be contracted to do jobs anywhere else.

Several other shops are on the ground floor of this building. On the west end is Propeller & Marine Service run by Christopher MacLean who does propeller reconditioning and re-pitching, precision shaft straightening and MIG and TIG welding. If your boat vibrates excessively while under power, your solution may be right here.

Cask Woodworking (VHF 69) is next door. They have a large selection of woods, veneers, plywood and counter surfaces. They can rebuild decks and interiors as well as freezer boxes and counter tops. Or they can plane, turn and cut stock for you. They have an extensive array of machinery as well as a kiln dryer and dustless varnishing room. Talk to Ansley Chang or Nick Adam.

Next to that is Ali's Machine Shop (VHF 68) Intiaz Ali can manufacture or repair almost anything out of stainless steel, bronze, brass and even titanium. From stainless steel shafts with a diameter of more than 6 inches and 40 ft long, to custom made toggles to fit your particular need. His precision machining tools can do the job. He also has in stock a wide selection of metric bolts and nuts in stainless steel.

Serge's Electrical Workshop (VHF 69) is right next door, he does boat wiring, motor and generator rewinding as well as supplying and installing deep cycle batteries.

Upstairs is Sail & Fly Travel Agency (VHF 68) besides arranging economical air travel and hotel accommodations, they do tours to Asa Wright Nature Centre, Caroni Bird Sanctuary and during March to June they will take you to the east coast to see the leatherback sea turtle lay her eggs in the sand, an unforgettable experience. They also offer a crew pool, fax, copy and office service. You can surf the internet on their computer or use their E-mail address to receive messages. If you are hauling out for the hurricane season you can fax or call them for your outgoing flight reservations well in advance since this is a busy period.

Convenient Rental Limited (VHF 68) is located in the same area. They have a 24 hr. service, offer a selection of vehicles with unlimited mileage by the day, week or month. They also help with advice on where to go, what to see and how to get there.

West Point Mini-mart (VHF 68) next door are open everyday including Sunday morning. They get daily deliveries of fresh Bagels and bread from Adam's Bakery and carry a wide selection of foods stuffs and drinks. They will deliver at no extra cost to any of the marinas in the area. No order is too small, just call it in. They have a book swap, gifts and crafts, and will even give you that day's weatherfax picture.

Also upstairs in the same building is Calypso Marine Canvas & Cushions (VHF 68) owned and operated by Riad Shakeer. Whether you need cushions, biminis, awnings or dodgers, Riad will make sure you get a good job. If your bunk cushions have become a little squishy, think about getting new ones here. They have fine high density foam, a wide selection of fabrics, and for extra comfort will laminate a thinner layer of the soft foam on the top. They do all their own pipe bending for biminis and dodgers, in both aluminum and stainless.

Carlos Marine Electronics (VHF 68) a wiz at electronics repair is next door. Before you give up on anything from your radar to your autopilot let him advise you on it. With over 25 years experience working in various fields of electronics including developmental work, he has the equipment and the know-how to solve your problem.

Also in Peake you will find Doug (VHF 72) who fabricates wind generators called Dougbuggers. These 3 bladers are constructed of fiberglass and can be made to match your yacht color. In the same shop is TMP Marine representing Isotherm refrigeration systems, a water cooled, 12 DCV, low draw type. They will install as well as service them and custom make the boxes for you.

Down the road west of Peake is IMS, Industrial Marine Services (VHF 68) who have a 70-ton travelift and capacity for about 130 boats on the hard. They have all the necessary services including showers, toilets, and washing machines and they sell tickets for the bus which passes outside. IMS it should be noted, also makes excellent paints, including epoxies and antifoulings, as well as a new poly siloxane, which renders a very tough topside finish and has the advantage of easy application with brush, roller or spray. Their Ameron antifouling comes in a copper base for glass and steel boats, or a tin base for aluminum hulls and is very effective in this environment. Their representatives in the yard can give you the best advise on preparation and application as well as help you do it, talk to Glen Stodart downstairs in their office.

Kent Johansson and his team operate Atlantic Yacht Services (VHF 68) and are the resident contractors in the yard. Kent, Nicklas, Tony and Bill all have extensive cruising experience and understand boats. One of them will be assigned to your boat as project manager to oversee all your needs, from traditional yacht wood repair to hull extensions in exotic materials. Or, if you prefer to do the work on your own, they can rent you tools and workshop space.

Ocean Sails Limited has a 2000 sq/ft loft on the south west side of the yard and is run by Michael Pegart who has 17 years of sailmaking experience backed by extensive cruising. He can repair and build any size sail, put on a UV cover on your roller furling jib, or make you an awning or complete boat cover. He carries a supply of sail hardware, represents Facnor and Profurl furling systems and Lee sails.

Across the bay to the southeast is the largest facility to date, called Crews Inn Marina and Boatyard (VHF 68). They boast the largest travelift in the region at 200-tons and have 63 in-the-water slips with water, telephone. T.V. and metered electricity. They regard these slips as hotel rooms, providing

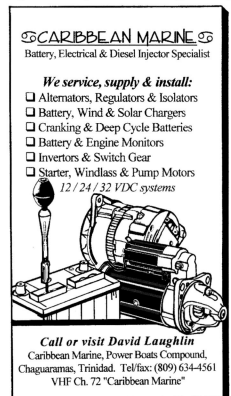

laundry, dry cleaning, food service and use of the pool and other facilities, and as befits this standard, exterior work on boats involving power tools is not allowed. When work is to be done, they have a huge converted bauxite shed with 2.7 acres under cover and 80 feet of vertical clearance. They can work on your boat even in the rainy season and in most cases without removing the rig. This is not a do-it-yourself yard and the hotel on the hillside will accommodate you while your job is being done.

Under the big roof you will find Dockyard Electrics Ltd. (VHF 68). They repair, maintain and install batteries, alternators, chargers, inverters and generators. And are also agents for Balmar alternators, Exide, Surrette, Prevailer and Rolls batteries, as well as Heart and Vanner inverters and chargers. Call them, they can come to you if you can't go to them. Richard and Susan Harmer Brown are the ones in charge.

Also here is Soca Sails (VHF 68) run by Mark Loe who can repair your sails or make awnings and boat covers. He also represents UK Sailmakers, well known for their Tape-Drive sails, and did some of his training at their loft in the US. To combat those harmful UV's that are so strong down here, have him sew a protective strip onto your roller furling jib.

Mercury and Mercruiser are represented by Bowen Marine. They can sell you a new outboard or their qualified mechanics can repair yours. They have been installing these engines on their own boats for years at their factory next to TTYA, so their experience is extensive.

The Quarterdeck is their general store and front desk, and is open 24 hours everyday. In addition to picking up those midnight snacks, you can arrange for a slip, get parts for your boat in the chandlery or browse in the boutique.

The lighthouse structure, just east of the docks, signals the location of The Village Square, where you can find customs and immigration, the restaurant and bar and 16 other stores and shops, including a bank, travel agency and bakery. This area has a dinghy dock and is separate from the slips to insure their privacy.

There is a narrow well protected creek that borders Power Boats to the east. To the other side, and as far up as you can go is Calypso Marine Services (VHF 68). They have been building fiberglass boats for over 25 years and specialize in pirogues and whaler types from 15 ft. to 32 ft. They do fiberglass repairs, woodwork and fix outboard engines. Their dock right at the workshop makes it convenient. If you want to try some deep-sea fishing on your own, you can rent a pirogue from them complete with a bimini for a very reasonable rate.

Stella Maris (VHF 68) is right next door, Harold LaBorde, famous Trinidadian sailor who has circumnavigated several times on the boats he has built, is the owner/operator of this dock facility. There is alongside space for about 5 boats with plenty of water depth, and being in this narrow creek affords maximum protection in the worst of conditions. A 200 foot dock is proposed, that will add more capacity for stern-to docking. Additionally Harold is the port officer for the Ocean Cruising Club. Facilities include, water, electricity store rooms and repair facilities.

Tardieu Marine (VHF 68) borders Stella Maris to the east. Run by Heather and Derrick, this yard stores and launches trailered powerboats as well as catering to cruisers at their two docks. Services include water, electricity, ice, toilets and showers. Two other businesses are in this yard. Yachtfitters (VHF 68), a procurement company, provides a regular shipping schedule which enables parts and materials to be imported in a cost effective manner. Regis Gouon and Dietmar Zuber do metal fabrication. Regis is the aluminum man and he built his own cruising boat from this material. Dietmar works in stainless steel and can fabricate or repair just about anything. Both are cruising folk with years of sailing experience.

Just down the road is the proposed Tropical Marine Ltd. They will have dockage space and fabricate fiberglass dinghies from 8 to 13 feet long as well as larger cruising catamarans. Teak and other lumber cut to order is available from them as well as woodwork and fiberglass repair. A chandlery is planned.

In addition to businesses with offices in the yards, there are contractors who work daily around the yards, but have their workshops elsewhere. You can call them on the phone or ask for them in Power Boats.

Allan Dowden of Yacht Maintenance Services is an invaluable resource. He does excellent spray painting and antifouling jobs,

and will look after your boat if you are going away, keeping it aired out and charged up. He is very reliable. Contact him on the phone. He works in both the Chaguaramas and Carenage areas.

Awon's Marine Services is headed by Gerald Awon who has many years experience in various types of finishes. You will find no one better at matching gel-coat and paint colors, so he is in great demand for gel-coat repair. He also does excellent topside and varnish spray painting using a High Volume Low Pressure method of spray application that eliminates costly use of excessive paint.

For a less high tech approach Akee (Carrington Donald) does a first rate varnish job with a brush, and Teepo (Clyde Bernard) does an excellent job of antifouling many of the boats in Power Boats.

For top quality, comprehensive electrical work contact Leslie Dookie of Marine Electrical Systems. With 25 years experience and training in both the US and UK, he is the man for complete wiring or re-wiring jobs or to diagnose your problem and rectify it no matter how complex.

There are also several businesses far from the yachting area that are well worth knowing about.

Trincity Chrome ltd. are best known for their chrome work which is very reasonable

and good quality. The mainstay of their business is chroming all the steel drums for carnival, so adding a few winches, stove parts, clocks and compasses is no problem. They also gold-plate and bronze-plate as well as polish and lacquer brass. Allow a couple of weeks for having things chromed, and if you don't want to ride out to Trincity, Peake and several of the other yards can arrange the work for you. Old finishes have to be removed before chroming, which they do for you, but they cannot remove baked-on enamel.

General Diesel are the people to contact for parts or replacement for Detroit Diesel, Allison Transmissions, Cummins, Delco Remy and other well known brands.

Marc One are the specialists for your polyester and epoxy supplies. Those doing an osmosis job might want to discuss their Duratec Vinylester system of protection. Marc One also sell power tools and inverters.

UA Weldequip carry several items of interest to those on yachts including Bosch power tools, grinding and sanding disks and they sell and refill fire extinguishers.

Cisl carry a modern range of insulating materials for all kinds of jobs from soundproofing the engine room to lagging the exhaust pipe. They will also survey your problem and advise on a solution.

Peter Pinheiro is the roving salesman representing Doyle Sails and if you call him he will come measure up your rig.

Berger produces an excellent line of paints, including a whole range for marine use and will be happy to advise you on your particular needs.

Need new mattresses? The easiest thing to do is visit one of the upholsters in the yard. But, for a bit of an adventure you can go visit the Lensyl factory in Trincity, buy your foam and have custom covers and even fitted sheets made. There are a few advantages to going yourself. They a have wide variety of different density foams and make several composite-type mattresses combining hard and soft foams. By going yourself you can find the one that suits you the best. They also have a big quilting machine that finishes the mattresses with a cover of two thin layers of foam and fabric for extra comfort - they can

CHAGUARAMAS ANCHORAGE

also do this on custom shapes. They can cut foam to absolutely any shape and angle, but keep in mind, that unlike the upholsterers they will not come to the boat to measure up, which means you would have to take along exact measurements or an old mattress for a pattern, and you would be responsible for getting the shape right.

If you would prefer to wash your old covers rather than make new ones, then Chin's laundry is the answer. They pick up and deliver free from all the marinas, and in most cases you just leave your dirty laundry in the marina office for the next collection.

Pet owners can get their supplies from the Dog House in Cocorite or Maraval.

Ashore

The Lifeline Bar (D), at Power Boats, opens seven days a week for breakfast, lunch, dinner and drinks. It is an inexpensive hangout for boat people and ideal for those working on their boats. The food is inexpensive and convenient enough that you might not want to bother cooking on the boat. Takeout service is available if you rather eat on board. Be there for their happy hour from 1800 to 1900 daily. On Mondays, starting at 1800, is a trivial pursuit contest. On some evenings live music is played by a guitarist or two. If you need a taxi you will often find Victor, a good and reliable driver, here. You can also call him at home.

A vegetable truck visits Power Boats every Wednesday and Saturday over lunch until about 1500, after which it moves on to Peake and then IMS.

At Peake check out The Bight (C-D), an indoor/outdoor restaurant and bar. It opens from 0800 onwards serving a wide variety of dishes including an excellent salad bar where you can pile up your plate high with fresh vegetables and tropical fruits. They also have a take out service for those on the move.

Nip'N'Tuck (D) at IMS, is open everyday except Sunday from 1000 onwards, although they are there from about 0800 and will whip you up a breakfast and coffee if you ask them. They serve some Chinese food as well as fish, chicken and pork dishes in addition to sandwiches. Friday's they have two happy hours, from 1600 to 1700, and then again from 1900 to 2000.

For a meal at CrewsInn, check out The Lighthouse Grub and Grog (C-D) run by Cleve and Carol, where you can dine outdoors in a tiki-village like atmosphere or a quieter air-conditioned room. Breakfast starts at 0700, be it continental or American. Seafood, steaks and specials are served for lunch and dinner, a daily happy hour is planned.

The Cove is at the western end of Chaguaramas. It is an apartment hotel that rents rooms as well as self contained cabanas by the day, week or month. If you are having extensive work done on your boat, this may well be a comfortable alternative to staying on board. Although they do not have air-conditioning, the cottages are set amongst the overhanging trees which provide a cooling shade, fans are provided as well as daily maid service. There is a restaurant and bar, beach and pool, a small minimart and boutique.

65

Water Sports

Ever thought of diving in Trinidad? True, you don't find the pretty reefs of Tobago, and visibility is often only 30-60 feet, but the fish life is fantastic with large groupers, huge lobsters, and massive schools of snappers and jacks. Rocky at Dive Specialist Center (VHF 68) runs a full Padi dive shop, offering same day filling, courses, equipment repair, bottle inspection and hydrotesting. If your onboard compressor breaks down, he is the man to see. He rents as well as sells scuba equipment and fishing gear. You will find him down at Cove Bay towards the western end of Chaguaramas, just before the road block to the military unit. If you go by sea, the dinghy dock is just after the sandy beach.

FANTASY ISLAND MARINA

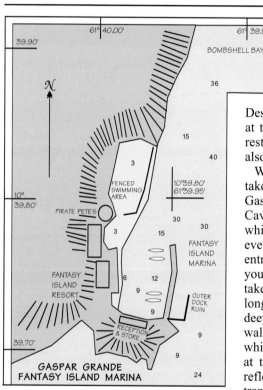

GASPAR GRANDE
FANTASY ISLAND MARINA

Desalinated water and electricity is available at the dock. There is a small minimart, a restaurant and bar, and a swimming pool, also a water slide and Tarzan leap for kids.

While you are anchored in Chaguaramas, take the side trip to the western side of Gaspar Grande Island to see the Gasparee Caves. The caves are within a large park which has walks and picnic tables. It is open every day from 0900 to 1430. For a small entrance fee ($5TT adults, $3TT children) you will be taken on a guided tour which takes about 20 minutes. You walk down a long staircase into the cave - about 100 feet deep and 200 feet across at the bottom. The walls and ceiling are hung with stalactites which form strange patterns. There is a pool at the bottom in which you can see the reflection of the trees overhanging the entrance high above. Fruit bats live in the ceilings and they venture out at night to eat wild balata fruits. The remains of their midnight snacks can be seen on the floor of the cave. In the park grounds there also are two large guns left by the Americans after World War II. There are good views from both sites.

To get there, dinghy down toward the far end of Gaspar Grande. Just before you get to the western tip you will see the public landing which has a small rest shelter and a notice board. Take a dinghy anchor and an extra line so you can anchor your dinghy clear of the access dock and tie it to the shore. Follow the clearly marked path.

On the eastern side of Gaspar Grande is Fantasy Island Marina Resort. A small breakwater offers good shelter for about 15 boats stern-to. Managed by David Weston and owned by Peter Easton, this is a quiet place to go to when you want to get away from the crowds and enjoy a more natural environment. There is a beach, some trails, more animal and bird life, as well as historic interest. You can even get off the boat and rent a room or whole cabana if you are tired of cramped quarters or have guests visiting. Communication to the mainland is serviced by a regular ferry and telephone service.

CARENAGE BAY

The normal route to Carenage Bay is between Point Gourde and the Diego Islands. The southern island was mined for an ingredient in the special cement that is used for capping oil wells. Current production is small. The northern island is a prison. You may be told that the long chute down into the sea is to take the heads of guillotined prisoners, but it is merely a drain.

Just before Carenage Bay, there is a good

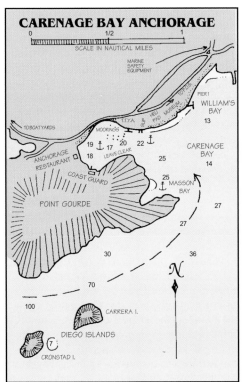

anchorage in Masson Bay in about 20 feet of water. This is out of any southerly chop, but can be affected in an northeasterly wind.

Carenage Bay is a popular anchorage in Trinidad, with easy access ashore via the Trinidad and Tobago Yachting Association (TTYA). There are many moorings off TTYA and they occasionally have some for rent. Otherwise, just anchor south of their moorings and make sure you are well dug in. Do not anchor too far in the south side of the bay, as the coast guard has a station here and will consider you to be in their way. If you have to anchor east of the moorings, due to lack of space, use two anchors, since the holding is not so good here. Make sure they are well set because there has been serious damage done by yachts dragging into the moored boats. This anchorage is usually beautifully calm, but when the wind comes south of east (most often in the spring) it creates an unpleasant surge which will cause you to pitch up and down during the day.

Pier 1 is to the northeast of TTYA. It has a 150-foot dock with 20 to 25 feet of water to accommodate the biggest of maxi yachts. Another dock just inland will accommodate smaller boats. They have water and electricity and diesel is planned. There is a restaurant, bar, pool and conference center. On some weekends they organize special functions that will introduce you to the real "trini" lifestyle.

Services

The TTYA (VHF:68) is open to visiting yachtspeople who have sailing yachts. Power boats are not accepted. Yachts on charter are also not accepted unless it is a yacht club charter and arrangements have been made in advance. It is a private yacht club, not a commercial establishment. A certain sensitivity is called for to keep the current excellent relationship between visiting yachtspeople and locals. The yacht club can comfortably accommodate about 20 visiting yachts normally and up to 30 during carnival. There are not usually this many visitors, but if you find the place packed with visiting yachts, think about going somewhere else until a few people leave. While you are here you should become a temporary or full member, depending on how long you are staying, temporary memberships can be for a week or a month, the rates are very reasonable, and it is a positive way to show your appreciation. Ask in the office for details. There is a small dock with electricity and water. Ashore there are showers, a laundromat, 2 card phones and one USA direct phone, a workshop, water and ice are available. They have full communications service and a photocopy machine, as well as FedEx and UPS service. If you don't want to do the laundry yourself, Chin's one day laundry and dry cleaning can be arranged through the office. There is a 15-ton travel lift, and although the area ashore is not huge, they do sometimes have room to store yachts. You can also haul for painting and repair. (See also the services in Chaguaramas.) You can use their dock to come alongside to take on water or get gear on and off. Arrange it in advance and make sure you do it on a weekday as it is in constant use by club members on weekends.

Marine Safety Equipment (VHF 68) is a 15 minute walk down the road toward Port of Spain. Look for a small road on the left after the larger junction. They repair and service all makes of liferafts and inflatable dinghies. They sell RFD Survivors, and Elliot liferafts, Plastimo and Cosalt safety gear such as life rings, jackets and flares. If your dinghy needs repair, you don't have to lug it around, give them a call, they will pick it up, and if it is beyond repair they can order you a new one within a few days.

For a pleasant taxi driver call Junior (VHF:68 "Locomotion"). or Ian taxi (VHF 68)

Ashore

The legendary hospitality of the TTYA has done much to encourage visiting yachts in Trinidad. When you arrive, walk upstairs to the office which opens at 1000, breaks an hour for lunch and reopens till almost 1700. See Claudette Jardine who will welcome you to Trinidad and give you a package of information about the island. Before long, you will think of this as your own club. For the carnival period they make a special effort to arrange things so that visitors can easily get to see the shows and be in all the right places

MOORINGS AT TTYA

at the right time. They also like to throw a fete and barbecue every Friday of the full moon. Being at the Yachting Association is a good way to get to meet some Trinidadian yachtspeople. Please bear in mind that if you have young children, do not leave them unattended on the grounds.

Windjammers (D) is the restaurant at TTYA and it opens from 0900 to 2000 daily except Mondays, The Spinnaker Bar is open daily to about 2200. In the office you can arrange rental cars, fast food, arrange for daily delivery of fresh bagels or bread from Adams, deliveries of large grocery orders, collection and delivery of laundry and cooking gas, buy phone cards or tickets for the bus to town, which runs about once every 1/2 hour.

The Anchorage restaurant (B-C, closed Sundays) is open to the sea and the breeze, with a deck right on the water where the lights at night bring in a variety of fish especially schools of catfish. The Anchorage has a Thursday and Friday afternoon lime with a happy hour from 1700 to 2100 followed by a DJ and live band. On Saturdays there is a live band that gets started at about 2200 to 2300 in true trini style. For dinner on any night they will be glad to pick up your party at any of the nearby yacht facilities and take you back, just give them a call.

Next to TTYA is The Chaguaramas Military History and Aviation Museum, displaying hundreds of air and wartime artifacts as well as documenting the role of Trinidad during the war.

Water Sports

TTYA is the home of yacht racing in Trinidad & Tobago and have races on a regular basis in both racing and cruising class. They also have a junior sailing school that uses Optimist dinghies to teach the young ones, so if you would like your son or daughter to learn the finer points of sailing and racing, consider enrolling them in the sailing school. There are several instructors on hand and they also run an intensive program during the summer months.

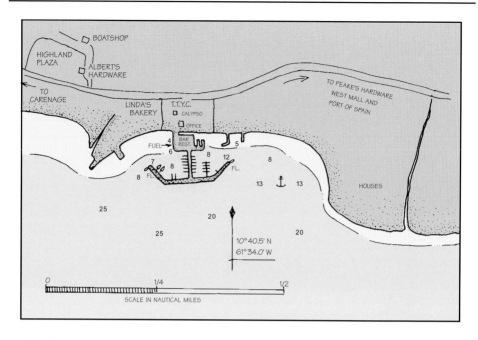

Like the TTYA, the TTYC, Trinidad & Tobago Yacht Club, is a private club. They welcome visitors, have good docks and operate a bit like a commercial marina. You pay a small fee to be a temporary member while you are here. You can also anchor off the Yacht Club and use the facilities by paying a reasonable temporary member's fee. The TTYC is full during carnival and advance booking for this period is essential. The marina is well protected and comfortable, though the outside anchorage is rolly in a southeast wind.

Services

Water and electricity (110/220 volt, 60 cycle), telephone, internet and cable TV are on the slips. Diesel and gas are available at the fuel dock. It is open weekdays 1000-1800 and weekends 0800-1600. Access to the fuel dock is a little difficult for boats over six feet deep, though dredging is planned. At least the bottom is mud. When you come into the west side of the dock, stay in the deepest water by shaving the pier wall as closely as possible. There are toilets and showers ashore. The office is open 0800-1800 Monday to Friday and 0800-1300 on weekends.

Inside full office services are available as well as phone cards and newspapers arrive every morning. Outside there are card phones and a USA direct phone, a laundromat, or you can use Chin's laundry and dry cleaning service which picks up and delivers.

In the Yacht Club you will see Calypso Marine Canvas Ltd. (VHF:68), who also have a workshop at Peake, and can make cushions from various density foams as well as dodgers and biminis using either stainless steel or aluminium tubing which they bend right there. They can also do scotch guard waterproofing on fabric.

Daco Air Conditioning and Refrigeration at Glencoe specializes in marine systems, installation, sales, service and repairs. So when things get too hot, or your system breaks down, give them a call. They will come and visit your yacht either at the Yacht Club or in Chaguaramas.

A mile or two down the road toward Port of Spain you come to Peake Hardware (VHF69), just after the West Mall. They are full sales and service agents for Johnson outboards. The hardware store is modern and inclusive with a selection of marine hardware, includ-

ing fittings, ropes, and accessories. They are agents for Stalok, Harken, Jabsco, Adler Barber and Crosby cooling systems. They also have an excellent selection of fishing, snorkeling, and diving equipment.

Peake are also major air-conditioning manufacturers. They rent a few air conditioners to yachts at a reasonable rate and are good people to consult if you need air-conditioning or refrigeration repairs. If they cannot do the job themselves, they can refer you to someone else.

If you need new batteries contact Lange Eighty with outlets in both San Fernando and Port of Spain. They keep a wide range of heavy duty batteries in stock.

Max Serrao keeps his yacht at TTYC and is the best man to see for electronic repairs. He fixes most kinds of VHF radios, all makes of autopilot, and will work on anything else if you have the circuit diagram.

Marine Hardware & Accessories in West Mall are the agents for Sea Recovery watermakers and Northern Lights generators. They can install, and service these and have a good range of spares. You will also find water pumps, ropes, stainless steel bolts and nuts as well as general hardware. If you want to clean out your diesel tank, they have a service that recirculates the diesel, passing it through a filter, removing all the moisture and sediment from your tank. This process lasts about 3 hours and is best done with 3/4 of the tank full of diesel, having previously

71

added Biobor to kill the fungus. You need to be on a dock with power. The parent company, C.E. Tang Yuk, started over 40 years ago in Port of Spain.

If cockroaches have been bugging you, or you want to leave your yacht out of the water and come back to it as uninhabited as you left it, then you can contact Rentokil.

Ashore

The TTYC has a restaurant and bar called Pisces on the Sea (D) managed by Annette Callander, and are open everyday from 0900 to 2130. Tuesdays is pizza night, Fridays, fish and chips and Saturdays for lunch they serve oxtail soup. Their regular menu covers everything from kingfish or shrimp to porterhouse or ribeye steaks. A variety of snacks are available with your drinks. For carnival they bring in a steel band for your entertainment.

Tours Incredible is operated by Annette's husband Arnold Callander who offers excursions to Asa Wright Nature Centre, Caroni Swamp, North Coast beaches and Turtle watch amongst others.

The TTYC is the best placed of all the main anchorages for getting around. It is on a direct and very frequent bus route to town. Next door to the marina is a branch of Linda's Bakery which opens 1000 to 1900, except on Saturdays when it opens an hour earlier (closed Sunday). A few steps away is the Highland Plaza. Here you can provision at Hi Lo Supermarket which is open daily from 0800-1900. On Fridays and Saturdays they stay open an hour later and on Sundays they close at 1300. They deliver orders of more than about $40US up to 1700. The Boat Shop is just north of the Hi Lo. This is a good general chandlery with fittings, tools, paint, electrics and anchors. In addition, they have a good selection of diving and fishing equipment, Julien Barton, the manager, is very helpful. Also of interest here is Glencoe Pharmacy, open 0900 to 1900 everyday and up to 1200 on Sundays; An auto supply store called Parts Unlimited; a video rental place; a Royal Bank 24 hr. Teller; a boutique called Heat Waves and fast food by Pizza Boys, Burger Boys and

Wok 'n Roll who will deliver.

Albert's Hardware has fishing gear, marine cleaners, sandpaper, brushes, and fittings. The manager, Susan Hadeed, is a member of the Yacht Club and helpful.

A few blocks west of the Yacht Club is L.P. Marine and Industrial Supplies Limited. They are the agents for Volvo Penta, Johnson Pump and G&M generators, and carry a very complete line of parts. Besides having impellers for all types of salt water pumps they can maintain and repair them in their workshop. They carry cutlass bearings, morse cables, filters, exhaust hoses, VDO instruments, fish finders, GPS's and much more. If you happen to be in Tobago and need something, give them a call, they have someone there that will deliver to you.

Right next door is The Tackle Shop for all your fishing needs, from Penn reels, to Rappala lures and everything in between plus some advice and local knowledge.

There are several large modern shopping malls a short drive away which will satisfy most of your needs. The nearest and most plush is West Mall with a Hi Lo Supermarket and a whole array of fancy shops. You can cool out here at Jardin des Tuileries, a cozy continental style tea house which serves French pattisseries and a wide range of teas. Moon over Bourbon Street (C-D) is an open air, patio style cocktail bar on the upper level of West Mall with a view over the sea. Good for a sundowner with a happy hour daily 1700 to 1800. Snacks and daily specials, including all the shrimp you can eat on Wednesdays, and live entertainment on weekends. Next door is Indigo (C-D) serving authentic east Indian food. For Chinese food in an intimate atmosphere try

Lychee Garden Restaurant (C) upstairs in the mall, open for lunch and dinner except Sunday.

Lazzari & Sampson Travel Service (VHF 68) is located downstairs in West Mall. They are a service-minded agency who handle not only your trip abroad but local excursions, tours to Venezuela, car rentals and visa assistance. They are the best people to speak to if you plan to travel with your pet. They have another office in town.

If it you cannot find what you want in West Mall, you can try the Starlite mall at Diego Martin. The Starlite laundry there is one of the cheaper places to get your wash done. For four floors of shops try the Long Circular Mall. There is a True Value Supermarket where the prices are reasonable and they take Visa cards.

Seabelle (C) in St. James is open 1100 to midnight Monday to Saturday. This restaurant is particularly famous for their crab backs. It is a hard place to find. No sign on the road, just the number 27 on the blue gates outside (27 Mucurapo Road). It is just across the road from Allai's and the Hot Shoppe. The Hot Shoppe, by the way, is famous for its rotis. In the same general area the Smoky and Bunty bar is a popular place with the young crowd looking for somewhere still open in the wee hours.

If you have rented a car it may take you a short while to become familiar with the roads. The following notes should help on your first sortie to the east to visit malls, etc. When you come out of the Yacht Club and turn right there are two flyovers not far down the road. For West Mall get in the right lane just before the first flyover and turn right. To go north to Diego Martin (or the Diego Martin Mall) take the left turn before the flyover. If you mess up and go over the flyover there is a right turn just after which will bring you back in the opposite direction.

The second flyover will take you on the back road through St. James to Port of Spain. To visit Peake or to take the faster Foreshore Freeway to Port of Spain, turn left just before the flyover. Pass under the flyover and turn left onto the Foreshore Freeway. Ideally, to get to Peake you would turn right on the Freeway as it is just down the road. However, this is not allowed, so as you come under the flyover keep to the left lane, take the first left off the main road, turn around and come back down the same road. Now you can turn in the right direction.

PORT OF SPAIN

Port of Spain is a lively bustling city full of color. The anchorage is very well protected, even in the southeasterly winds that make the other anchorages rolly. However, you need to take precautions against theft. Lock your boat up well during the day and leave someone on board after dark. Many boats anchor here during carnival time when all the anchorages get crowded.

Navigation

As you approach Port of Spain two tall twin buildings stand out from afar. These are the country's financial center and were opened in 1985.

The water off Port of Spain is shallow and full of wrecks for about a mile out. It is best to stay in 30-40 feet of water until you link in with the main dredged channel. Follow this in and anchor near the small docks.

Note also the commercial fishing channel to the southeast of Port of Spain. You would not normally enter here, but in the unlikely

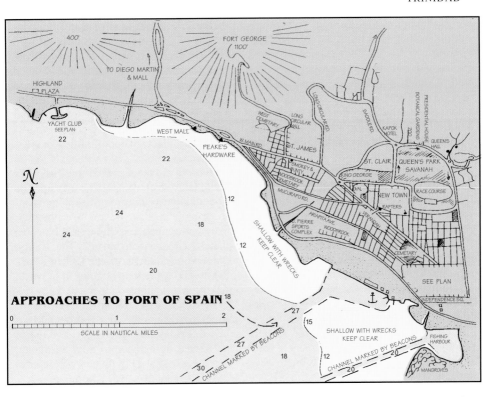

APPROACHES TO PORT OF SPAIN

SCALE IN NAUTICAL MILES

event of a bad storm or hurricane, it would be one of the more secure spots.

Regulations

Port of Spain is a commercial port of entry. Yachts should check in at Chaguaramas.

Services

Marine Consultants Ltd. keeps a good stock of charts and cruising guides. They are also compass adjusters and sell and service safety equipment, including flares, life jackets, EPIRBS and GPS. They are agents for Tideland, Viking and Beaufort liferafts and inflatable dinghies. They also service liferafts and inflatables.

If you want to leave your boat here and travel or arrange for something to be shipped in, you will get help at Lazzari and Sampson (VHF:68) on Pembroke Street. Lazzari and Sampson are a complete travel agent and under the name Piarco Air Services they handle all air freight.

Ashore

The nearest supermarket is Lue Shue on Independence Square. You will also find plenty of food down Charlotte Street where open fruit, vegetable and fish stalls line the road.

There are two big general hardware stores that are fascinating to browse in and where you are bound to find something you need. Trestrails is on Broadway just off Independence Square and William Scott is farther east on Independence Square. Scott carries brand names like Makita tools, Coleman, Ridgid and Stanley. They have also a good selection of lumber and plywoods.

If you lost your glasses overboard, you might want to visit Ferreira Optical on Frederick Street. They have the latest in equipment, can examine you and make new glasses at a good price. Bring in your diving mask too, and they will put in your prescription, or for those of us who need some magnification they can put in a magnifying lens on the bottom half of the mask.

Radica Trading on Henry Street has a complete line of fabrics including upholstery materials, Sunbrella and real leather, foam rubber and plastic zippers of all sizes. Also nylon strapping, plastic snaps, brass grommets and stitching tools as well as 3M plastic non-skid matts in various sizes and colors.

Among other attractions, Port of Spain has the Emperor Valley Zoo. This was built in 1952 is and named after a large butterfly. It is well maintained and houses a good collection of Trinidad's wildlife species, along with a somewhat random collection of animals from other parts of the world. If you are coming by car there is parking space just west of the zoo.

The Botanical Garden, laid out in 1820, is one of the oldest in the western hemisphere. It is not as well cared for as the zoo, but it is worth walking across to look at the president's splendid house.

The Magnificent Seven are a group of eccentric and ostentatious residences. Six were built in 1904 when profits from cocoa plantations were high. One now is a college, another houses the offices of the prime minister.

If, after your tour of the town, you want to see all those great shots you took, get your film processed at Dalla Costa's Film Processors on Sackville Street.

Eating out can be as simple and inexpensive as visiting a Doubles salesmen who you usually see downtown around 1000. Doubles are sort of crepe with curried channa (chick peas) in them. Unless you like food the hottest of the hot, don't take the pepper. Rotis are also excellent in Port of Spain and make a good lunch.

There are plenty of opportunities for more gastronomic dining. Tiki Village (C) is on the top story of the Kapok Hotel. Just walk in and take the elevator all the way up. The air-conditioned dining room has picture windows and a bird's eye view over the city. They serve appetizing Chinese/Polynesian dishes at reasonable prices. The Kapok Hotel is on Saddle Road near Queen's Park and as Tiki Village is popular, it is worth making reservations.

Phyllis Viera's Verandah (C-D) is on Rust Street in a residential area. It is open Mondays to Fridays for lunch only, and meals are served on a spacious cool verandah. Parking is easy and Phyllis serves fine local food.

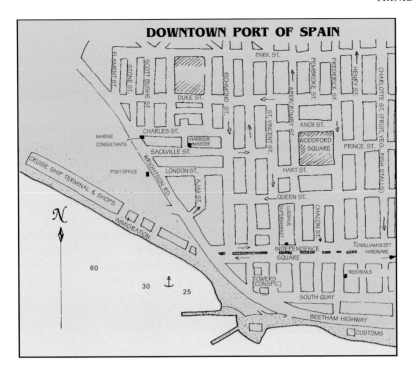

Rafters (C-D) is in an old stone and wood building that was originally a grocery store and has plenty of atmosphere. They open daily from 1145, except Sunday when they are closed. On public holidays they open in the evenings only. Go early for lunch as it becomes very busy. Rafters is air conditioned, classy and serves such delights as shrimp flambeaux, lobster Casablanca and filet Oscar. Pub food and snacks are also available.

Outside the Pelican Inn Pub is a big sign "Open any day anytime including public holidays." Inside it has an interesting sub- terranean atmosphere and the feeling of a British pub. This is a popular place and it attracts a band of regulars. They serve pub food such as steak and kidney pie.

The Hilton Hotel, just to the northeast of Queen's Park, is another cool oasis when the heat of the day gets to you. Picture windows in the restaurant look out over Port of Spain toward Carenage Bay. It is sometimes called an upside down hotel because the car park is at the top and the rooms are below. Their Sunday buffet is the bargain of the week.

The Hilton's main restaurant, La Boucan (A-B), offers buffets three nights a week with

entertainment, including a Friday poolside barbecue with a steel band. On Wednesday and Friday afternoons they serve tea.

For good Chinese food try the Panda Palace (C), at #5 Maraval Rd. open everyday for lunch and dinner. Their lemon chicken is recommended.

There are a number of good restaurants just outside Port of Spain in the direction of the yacht club.

Woodford Cafe (C) on Tragarete and Woodford St. is a delightful restaurant serving a good variety of seafood, meats and local dishes in pleasant surroundings. They are open for lunch and dinner, closed Sundays.

Inexpensive Rotis and Indian food in a more fast food setting can be had a few doors away at the Monsoon (D) on the corner of Tragarete and Picton St.

Le Chateau De Poisson (B) on the corner of Ariapita Ave. and Cornelio St. in Woodbrook, is a charming restored house left over from the days when that whole area was a flourishing sugar estate. A small garden surrounds

the house and hanging ferns bring the outdoors in. Colorfully dressed staff provide excellent service to match the quality of the seafood.

For something a little different, try Ali Baba on Saddle Road in Maraval. They offer a delightful range of Middle Eastern fare.

There is plenty of entertainment in Trinidad. The Queen's Hall will please classical buffs with concerts and ballet. They occasionally put on classical steel band music. They are most active around Christmas and Easter. Calypso shows, popular shows and big visiting artists are either at the National Stadium in the Jean Pierre sports complex or in the stands at the Queens Park Savannah locally known as "The Big Yard." The north stand is for the hard drinking set out to have a good time; the south side is for serious listeners.

CAIMAN

NORTHWEST TRINIDAD

When the partying and sightseeing become too much and you want to get away from it all, Trinidad has several delightful and quiet anchorages within easy reach. They are often deserted during the week, but are well used for local outings on weekends and holidays.

SCOTLAND BAY

This beautiful bay winds back into the hills like a fiord. It is often used as a last stop on the way to Tobago.

During the Second World War the Americans built a large recreational center here for their troops. The ruins of these are the only signs of habitation you will see. The water is generally very deep and when it does become shallow, it does so fast. The best anchorage is right up at the head of the bay in about 35 feet of water.

This is a pleasant place to sit and enjoy the view of the hills and the ample bird life. Corbeaus wheel overhead and fight on the beach, swallows sometimes rest on your lifelines and you can spend hours with binoculars trying to figure out which birds are making all the raucous sounds ashore. When sitting palls, don your snorkeling gear and check out the reefs near the island at the entrance.

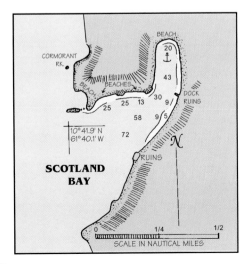

SCOTLAND BAY

MORRIS BAY

Morris Bay has no roads, but there are many holiday homes built right on the waterfront. These are reached by boat and the land and houses are all private. You can anchor here, but there is not much to do ashore.

Most of the bay is very deep but there is a good anchorage area up toward the head of the bay before it gets too shallow. Give good clearance to the 6-foot shoal off the south end of Blanchette Point. It is surrounded by very deep water and pops up suddenly.

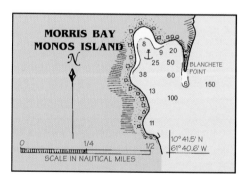

GRAND FOND BAY

This lovely bay is very quiet; there are just a few holiday homes dotted along the shore. Most of the bay is deep, but there is good anchorage in about 25 feet off the old pilings left over from World War II toward the head of the bay. The water shelves rapidly beyond the pilings. This anchorage seems well protected even when southeasterly winds are making boats roll in Chaguaramas.

You sit here surrounded by the hills and exotic songs from the birds ashore who generally manage to stay hidden in the

MORRIS BAY

trees. The beach at the head of the bay is covered in coconut palms, and makes a good spot for a barbecue. You can walk around the beach and a short way into the forest.

CHACACHACARE

Until about 30 years ago Chacachacare was a leper colony. It was a major community with a good sized village and a road running all around, busy enough to require a traffic light. When a cure for leprosy was found, the colony was abandoned. Many household and personal items were left where they were last used. Nature is about half way to reclaiming the buildings. It makes fascinating exploring, though you may need a cutlass to get through the bush from time to time.

The lighthouse up the hill is manned and you can walk up by following the road from the lighthouse dock. If you show interest, there is a good chance the keepers will invite you to take a tour.

La Tinta Bay on the west side has a pleasant beach and is popular on holidays.

Navigation

Chacachacare Bay affords excellent cruising. There are many anchorages and you can be sure to have one to yourself, except possibly on weekends. The wind tends to blow from the southeast or the northeast so one side is often more protected and you have to be prepared for a change in wind direction. The bay is very deep, and when it shelves it does so rapidly. The distance between anchoring depth and aground may be less than 100 feet. Therefore it pays to approach any anchorage cautiously. In some places with a rapid drop off, two anchors or a stern line ashore may be necessary.

The doctors' houses lie in two lovely little secluded bays. The shelf here is very steep, but stern-to anchoring is possible. Sanders Bay probably offers the best all-round anchorage. There is a wide enough shelf to anchor on in depths of 10 to 25 feet. Note the old sea road that runs around the rocks into Coco Bay. Coco Bay also offers a shelf where you can anchor. The landing stage for the lighthouse is at the south end of Perruquier

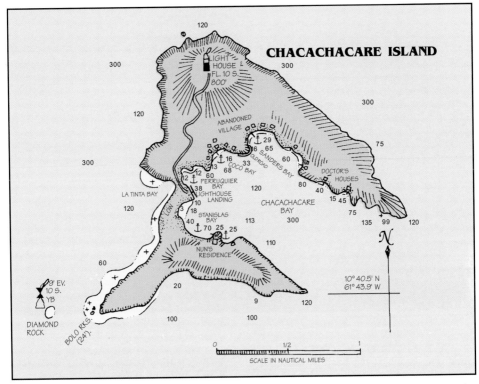

CHACACHACARE ISLAND

LIGHT HOUSE FL. 10 S. 800'

ABANDONED VILLAGE

SANDERS BAY

COCO BAY

OLD ROAD

PERRUQUIER BAY

LA TINTA BAY

LIGHTHOUSE LANDING

STANISLAS BAY

CHACACHACARE BAY

DOCTOR'S HOUSES

NUN'S RESIDENCE

DIAMOND ROCK

BOLO RKS. (24')

9' EV. 10 S. YB

10° 40.5' N
61° 43.9' W

0   1/2   1
SCALE IN NAUTICAL MILES

Bay. North of the dock are two secluded beaches. You could comfortably anchor here with one line in the deep water and another back in the shallows. Avoid the west end of Stanislas Bay as it is shoal. At the south end the water is very deep and the holding is bad, but once hooked, you can take a line to the dock. The little bay to the east of Stanislas Bay has pretty cliffs and a good anchoring shelf. It is eight feet most of the way to the shore.

There is a very small harbor on the south side of Gaspar Grande called Winns Bay. A big fig tree grows on the small rocky island at the entrance to the bay. The bay shelves rapidly, the holding is not great and the wind can come from any direction. However, if you anchor toward the center and put a line ashore to a tree you can get comfortable enough for an overnight stop.

As on many of the islands, there is nowhere to walk ashore, and there are just a few privately owned houses. This is a good place to hear kiskadees which call to each other across the bay. Though common in Trinidad and South America, this bird is not found in Tobago. French people hear it saying "Qu'est-ce-qu'il dit", and English hear it saying "Kiskadee". It is somewhat raucous in either language.

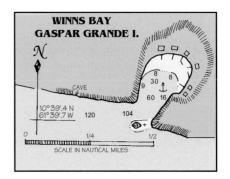

POINT-A-PIERRE

Pointe-a-Pierre is a few miles north of San Fernando in the southwestern portion of Trinidad, about 25 miles from the northern yacht anchorages. This area is quite industrialized. During the period of high oil prices in the early 1970's some of the income was

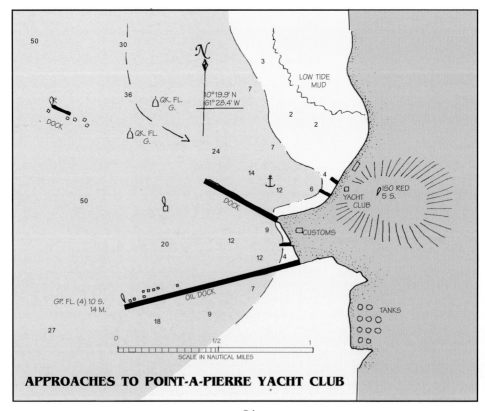

APPROACHES TO POINT-A-PIERRE YACHT CLUB

invested in a big industrial development at Port Lisas, just north of Pointe-a-Pierre. More recently the island has had to struggle to adjust to lower oil revenues.

The Pointe-a-Pierre Yacht Club is part of the Pointe-a-Pierre oil refinery. Despite this it is set in a peaceful scenic bay which is well protected. The Pointe-a-Pierre Wildfowl Trust is outstanding and this is an excellent anchorage from which to explore southern Trinidad. Best of all, the local yachtsmen love to see a new face, so you can be sure of a great welcome.

Navigation

The western shores of Trinidad are shoal a long way out, so stay four or five miles offshore or in at least 30 feet of water. Oil rigs, pipes and wrecks are features of the west coast, so it is best to go in daylight. As you come down the coast you will see Port Lisas, a huge industrial complex with chimneys, buildings and probably smoke about five miles north of Pointe-a-Pierre. Another good landmark is San Fernando Hill, a lone, oddly shaped hill in San Fernando. It looks like it does because parts have been sculpted by mining.

As you get closer you can see the two long docks at Pointe-a-Pierre; the southern one is a mile long. As you come in from the north, merge with the channel into the northern dock. Follow the dock down toward the yacht club and anchor in about 12 feet off the southern yacht club dock.

Regulations

Pointe-a-Pierre is a port of entry. You can anchor off the yacht club and walk or dinghy over to the customs shed which is at the head of the docks.

Services

Rod Gibbon, a yacht club member, works in teak. He makes a line of teak fittings which are resold through chandleries, but he is also a good choice if you wish to have cabinets, tables or custom teak work done on your boat.

Ashore

The yacht club bar is open Wednesday and Friday evenings and Saturday and Sunday afternoons. Drinks are very reasonable. You will probably be made a temporary member of the Pointe-a-Pierre Club which will enable you to use the other club facilities (open every day), including tennis courts, swimming pool, golf course and the main club restaurant and bar. The local members will make you feel right at home.

For trips to San Fernando or the Wildfowl Trust you can catch a maxi taxi right outside the gate.

The Pointe-a-Pierre Wildfowl Trust was started from within the refinery and is on its grounds. Its 60 acres include two lakes which are used as reservoirs for the refinery's cooling system. It was started in 1966 and now houses a captive breeding program where birds such as anhingas and scarlet ibises have recently hatched out. The lakes attract countless birds, including many ducks, geese, herons, storks and song birds. Look for gallinules and jacanas walking on the lily pads. Caimans can also be seen in the lakes. It is a wonderful place for a picnic and a good way to get acquainted with local and migrant birds. There is a nominal entrance fee and you have to call them in advance and let them know you are coming. Speak to Molly Gaskin.

Pointe-a-Pierre is ideally situated to explore Trinidad's southern forests, the east coast beaches and the pitch lake. Rental cars are available in San Fernando. There are also supermarkets, roti huts and pizza shacks in the San Fernando area, and Harry's Store is within walking distance of the club.

NORTH COAST OF TRINIDAD

The north coast of Trinidad has two reasonable anchorages which are useful as stopping places on the way to Tobago. This is an area to explore during the day in good light conditions so you can eyeball your way into the anchorages.

This is a spectacularly beautiful anchorage set in the wilds, amid steep wooded hills with a view back over Les Boqets and Saut d'Eau Islands. It is also the best north coast anchorage. You would be comfortable here for a day or two on your way to Tobago.

Navigation

As you approach along the north coast you can go between Saut d'Eau Island and Medine Point. Stay on the Medine Point side of the channel as there are some nasty looking rocks just below the surface (water breaks on them) just southeast of Saut d'Eau Island. Pass outside Les Boqets Islands and head over to the eastern side of La Vache Bay, below the Timberline Resort buildings.

You will see two small beaches with ruins near them. The best anchorage is off the northern of these beaches. There is a fair-sized shelf with good holding sand in 13-25 feet of water. As the wind comes from all directions in here, you may be safest and most comfortable with two anchors, holding your boat with bow or stern toward the beach.

Ashore

This is a great place for dinghy exploration among interesting caves, ledges and cliffs. In times of rain you can take your dinghy under a little waterfall dropping into the sea.

A trail leads from the ruin above the beach to Timberline Resort above. This is a great restaurant and bar perched on a ridge with spectacular views. Call in advance to make sure it will be open.

In a little house on the waterfront to the south of the anchorage you will find Frank McCume, who takes people on fishing trips and to explore nearby caves.

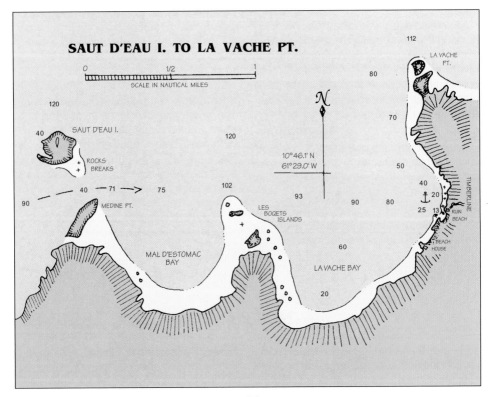

SAUT D'EAU I. TO LA VACHE PT.

MARACAS BAY

This magnificent bay is over a mile wide and has three white sand beaches. It is a very popular beach area for locals, especially on weekends and holidays. You will roll a little in here unless conditions are exceptionally calm, but it makes a perfectly acceptable rest stop on your way to Tobago. It has the advantage of being three miles farther east than La Vache Bay. I would consider this to be the last reasonable overnight anchorage along this coast, though in calm conditions it is also possible to anchor just inside Chupara Point, five miles farther up the coast.

Navigation

Pass outside the little island off Point Morro and head toward the east side of Maracas Bay. You will find a large shelf on which to anchor off the beach and close to the rocks. The holding is good in mud. Small swells come in from every direction, so a stern anchor is not much of a help. The wind, too, can switch around.

Ashore

This is a popular holiday spot and if you pull your dinghy up the nearest and calmest beach, you can walk west down the road to a big car park where some little shacks usually sell beer and snacks.

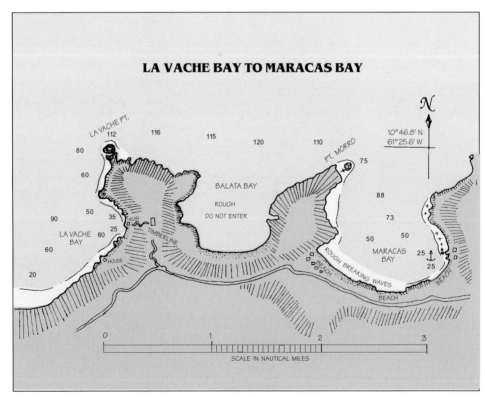

LA VACHE BAY TO MARACAS BAY

TOBAGO

Regulations

Trinidad and Tobago are one country. If you are coming from Trinidad and going to return to Trinidad before clearing out, there are no formalities. If you are coming from abroad you must first visit Scarborough with your yacht to check with customs and immigration. Similarly, when you leave Tobago for another country, you must return to Scarborough with your yacht to clear out. If you cleared into Tobago, and are going on to Trinidad, to leave from there, you must notify immigration so that they can send the papers to Trinidad in preparation for your clearance. If you plan to discharge any crew you must also notify immigration of those plans. Scarborough is about a three-hour beat from Crown Point against wind and current and about five or six hours from Man of War Bay. The procedures are easy once you arrive. If you want to avoid overtime charges (around $20 US), clear in weekdays 0800-1600. When you clear in let the customs officer know all the harbors you wish to visit.

The whole of Buccoo reef is now a restricted area and yachts are not allowed to anchor here. This restricted area may soon be expanded to include Buccoo Bay to the east.

Shopping hours

Shopping hours are 0800-1200 and 1300-1630. Most shops close Saturday afternoons and Sunday. Most banks open 0900-1400 Monday to Thursday and on Fridays 0800-1200 and 1500-1700.

Holidays

See Trinidad.

Telephones

There are card phones all around Tobago. Cards may be purchased at the National Canadian Bank, the TSTT building on the corner of Main and Jerningham Streets in Scarborough, at the tourist bureau or the Republic Bank at the airport, as well as various other locations. You cannot use card phones to make credit card or collect calls, but TSTT has a USA direct line, and there is one at the airport. See also Trinidad.

Transport

Tobago is connected to the rest of the Caribbean by LIAT and other airlines. There are several flights a day to Trinidad and you can link there with major airlines. There is a $75TT departure tax which you probably can avoid if you are leaving directly from a yacht.

Most people get around in "route taxis" which are normal size cars, or maxi taxis which are mini buses. Both have a license plate that begins with an H. (Note that regular taxis also begin with an H.) The fares range from $2TT for a short drop to about $12TT which would take you from Scarborough to Charlotteville. You flag down a taxi going in your direction, confirm the destination and fare and share the cab with other people who are doing the same thing. Route taxis will often also act as regular taxis and are often quite negotiable on price.

There are also individuals with private cars, whose license plate begins with a P, that provide a transport service and whose prices are close to those of the route taxis.

Regular taxis are also available and typical rates for 1-4 people in $US are:

5-6 hour trips......................$100
Scarborough to the airport .. $ 25
Scarborough to Plymouth......$ 25

There is also a bus system which runs throughout the island. The main bus terminal is in Scarborough near the market. Passengers must buy bus tickets in advance. Buses will not stop at the designated stops unless you stretch out your hand to signal them.

Rental cars are available and you can drive on a USA, UK or International license. Drive on the left.

TOBAGO

Tobago is a little out of the mainstream of the other Caribbean Islands. Too far to sail in a day and too often a struggle against wind and current, it is less popular than the islands to the north. However, for the adventurous sailor the extra effort required is amply rewarded by a visit to one of the last completely unspoiled Caribbean islands.

Tobago is a small (116 sq. miles) mountainous island with lovely beaches and green hills. With a population of only 47,000, it does not feel in the least bit crowded. Long used as a holiday place for Trinidadians, Tobago has a low key but expanding tourist industry. Fishing is important and much of the catch comes from seine netting. When anchoring in Tobago, you need to consider the needs of the fishermen. We give more details under specific anchorages where it is relevant.

Tobago changed hands between Dutch, English, Courlanders and French more times than any other Caribbean Island and the count is sometimes 24 times, sometimes 31. This figure is vague because for many years no country had a firm grasp on Tobago and a change in administration was hardly noticeable. (Who's counting?) Possibly spotted by Columbus in 1498, there was no permanent settlement for over 150 years. Carib raids and disease ended a Dutch settlement which was established in 1628. Later, colonists of various nationalities periodically laid waste to each other's settlements which disrupted the pirates operating in the area. The Duke of Courland (now part of Latvia) was very persistent in trying to exercise sovereignty over the island, which had been given to him as a birthday present by his godfather, King Charles II of England.

By 1771 English colonists were using slaves to grow and harvest sugar cane. After an infestation of ants destroyed the cane, the settlers tried cotton. In 1781 the French took the island over for 12 years and made serious attempts to develop Tobago's economy, still using slave labor to grow both sugar and cotton. After the British regained control in 1793 they remained in power with only a slight interruption until Trinidad and Tobago became an independent country in 1962. Tobago was united with Trinidad in 1899, after its economy had totally collapsed and no one knew what to with it.

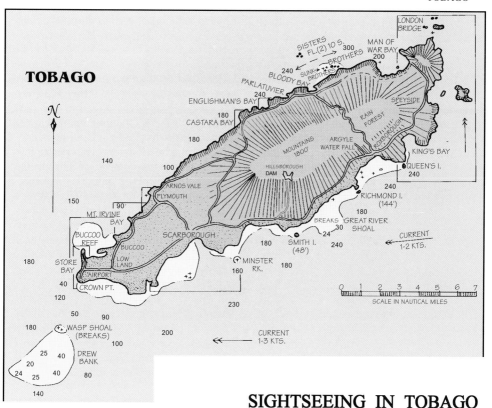

SIGHTSEEING IN TOBAGO

Tobago is an especially rewarding island for nature lovers. Like the Eastern Caribbean to the north, it has rain forests, clear waters and pristine beaches, but it is the only island apart from Trinidad that was once part of the South American continent. It has 210 species of nesting birds, whereas there are fewer than 80 on any other small island. Many of the birds are brightly colored and so unafraid that you can spot them from a car. After a while, if a bird doesn't have more colors than a traffic light, you hardly bother to look.

Strangely, Tobago shares several species of frogs, lizards and birds with South America which are not present in Trinidad. This has led to speculation that there was once a land bridge from Tobago to other parts of South America that skirted Trinidad. Trinidad was part of South America as recently as 11,000 years ago, but Tobago has not been part of the continent for more than a million years.

The cocrico, more properly the rufous-vented chachalaca, is Tobago's national bird. It is a big bird that looks a bit like a slender long tailed turkey. The raucous cries of "cocrico" begin at dawn, continue irregularly through the day and reach a second crescendo near dusk. The bird is protected by law but the din, together with its habit of eating some agricultural crops and the fact that it is quite tasty, have contributed to the perception that it is a pest. The birds are quite unwary and could quickly go from pest status to endangered species if unrestricted hunting were allowed.

There are two excellent outfits that lead nature tours in Tobago. David Rooks leads two scheduled nature trips each week and will arrange other journeys on request for four or more people. Every Thursday he takes groups to the bird sanctuary on Little Tobago Island and on Saturday his destination is the 14,000-acre protected rainforest in the center of the island. On both days other stops are included and you will learn about local agriculture and history as well as natural history. He is an enthusiastic and knowledgeable naturalist and birder, who is called in when the big wigs arrive. All-day tours cost $45 to $55US. Wear reasonably good walking shoes for the rainforest

trip and a change of clothes during the rainy season, June to December. The walk is only a couple of miles long but the path can be slippery. He will pick you up from most anchorages or arrange transportation from Man of War Bay or Tyrrel's Bay. On Tuesdays at 1730 he gives a lecture and slide show on Tobago's natural history at the Turtle Beach Hotel, Great Courland Bay.

Pat Turpin and Renson Jack operate Pioneer Journeys, an organization that specializes in exploring "the unknown Tobago." Pat's specialty is ferns and Renson is a forest warden, but they both know all aspects of their island's natural history thoroughly. Their four standard journeys each have a different focus and include visits to a cocoa plantation, the rainforest, a waterfall and wetlands for birdwatchers. On any trip you will see a good cross section of Tobago's natural history. Prices for full day tours range from $42 to $55US and include transport, meals and park fees.

If you are touring Tobago on your own, the prettiest roads are in the eastern half of the island, from Castara east on the north coast and from Roxborough round to Charlotteville. The road from Roxborough to Bloody Bay is right through rainforest, much of which has been protected since 1765. There are trails along this road which

PIGEON POINT

ARGYLE WATERFALLS

include a two-mile loop trail near the summit or a hike from the top down to Bloody Bay. There is a very rough road from Bloody Bay to Charlotteville. It is currently passable with a four-wheel drive, but might be better done as a hike. Two sets of waterfalls might attract your interest. The Argyle waterfalls at Roxborough are photogenically arranged in three tiers. There are pools for swimming and falls where you can take a shower. They are well sign-posted and there is a small fee to get in. You do not need a guide but the trained guides are not expensive and they are knowledgeable about the local trees and plants.

Rainbow waterfall at Goldsborough is signposted off the main road. It lies on the private land of Hugh McKenna. McKenna will be happy to give you a guided tour, you can also pay a reasonable fee (about $3 US pp) and he will put you on the right path. It is a delightful 15 minute walk through trees and meadows with big stands of bamboos and small patches of bananas. The fall is magnificent in the rainy season, more of a trickle in the dry season but at all times the pool below is delightful to swim in. If you come at a crowded time and prefer somewhere more private, McKenna can direct you to another fall which is a considerably longer walk. He is also planning a bar and restaurant.

Looking at a map of Tobago the Hillsborough Dam stands out bright blue against the land. Although not mentioned in any tourist literature it looked alluring so we paid a visit. parrots and kingfishers livened our drive along the twisty road and when we arrived we paid a nominal entry charge and signed the visitors book. We were the only visitors in a week. We were entranced by the pretty lake and the wildlife including cormorants, anhigas and herons. Best of all we got to see several of the small wild alligators (caiman) both swimming and sunning themselves on the bank. Take good binoculars. I am told the best bird watching is in the late afternoon.

As a break from all your driving, Richmond Great House (C-D) makes a magnificent lunch or drink stop. It lies in the hills above the south coast main road about 3 or 4 miles west of Roxborough. The gardens are replete with bearing fruit trees including cashews and avocados. A swinging seat affords a birds eye view over the swimming pool to the ocean in the distance. The estate house itself has been beautifully restored with lots of antiques and Afro-art. For those who want a real night away from the boat they have 10 rooms.

Heritage Festival

Beginning in mid-July and continuing until early August is Tobago's Heritage Festival, an annual celebration of the island's cultural and artistic history. The opening day's events take place at the cultural center in Shore Park, but then the center of activity moves from village to village each day. A boat is christened in the old way at Black Rock and then old style music, food, dances, even traditional ways of courting and marrying are re-lived, first in one village and then in the next.

Angostura Yachting World Regatta

A great way to see Tobago is to join in this premier yachting event sponsored by Angostura Rum and Yachting World Magazine. With plenty of fun for serious racers and laid-back cruisers alike. Live-aboards are specially catered to and you can be sure of enjoying plenty of good parties. This week long series of four races will take you to two anchorages and is usually held sometime in the earlier part of May.

Bumboat Races

Stick around for a week and you can see the local "Bumboat" races, held at Store Bay. These are the local sail powered fishing boats of yesteryear and attract competitors from as far away as Carriacou and Bequia.

NAVIGATION

Though just outside the "hurricane belt," Tobago has been hit. In 1847 a hurricane blew the roofs off the buildings at Fort King George. Hurricane Flora, an intense storm that struck in 1963, almost laid waste to the island's agricultural base.

Lying as it does at a slight angle to the trade winds, Tobago does not have an obvious windward or leeward shore. Anchorages are to be found in protected areas and indentations all around. How well protected these are depends on the prevailing conditions. The anchorages from Crown Point to Man of War Bay will be uncomfortable to untenable in any northerly swells. However, Tobago is small enough that it only takes a few hours to get from the north to the south coast. Inside the new harbor wall, Scarborough is comfortable in nearly every condition. The best time to come is from February onwards, when the chances of northerly swells and strong northeasterly winds have diminished. If you are planning to circumnavigate the island, it makes sense to go clockwise from Scarborough since the northern shore is generally more protected and has less current.

The tidal range is around three feet in Tobago, so when you anchor make sure you have enough water under your keel.

Although the waters around Tobago are generally clear they often become murky after heavy rainfall or if swells have stirred up the bottom. In addition outflow from the Orinoco can reduce undersea and reef visibility from time to time. This happens most often during the hurricane season, from August to October.

SCARBOROUGH

Scarborough has a tumultuous past. It was first settled by the Dutch Lampsin brothers and called Lampsinburg. Both the name and controlling power changed repeatedly from 1666 to 1803 when the British took the island from the French for the last time.

Today Scarborough is a lively town for its 17,000 inhabitants. People may tell you that Tobago is a calm and quiet backwater, the perfect antidote for the hectic pace of Trinidad. However, if you arrive in Scarborough on a Friday or weekend you will be greeted by a whole week's worth of cheerful noise, with the population relaxing in the town's streets. Every other restaurant blasts music into the air and people are laughing, walking, talking and selling food and trinkets from tiny stalls.

The new outer harbor wall makes Scarborough a protected anchorage and a good place to leave your boat while you explore the interior of the island.

Scarborough, the main town on Tobago, is naturally divided into two areas. An older section, Upper Scarborough, is on hilly ground to the east of the harbor. To the north of the harbor is Lower Scarborough, with a large new cruise-ship and ferry dock with terminal, a modern market building, bus station, library and shopping mall, along with an assortment of small enterprises. A large, conspicuous pink building stands out in Lower Scarborough, about a five minute walk beyond the cruise ship dock.

Navigation

Scarborough is upwind and current of anywhere you might come from, unless you make this your first landfall when crossing the Atlantic. A current of one to two knots sweeps westwards along the coast and right the way over to Trinidad. It is only about nine miles from Crown Point to Scarborough but it can take about three hours motor sailing against wind and current to get there. If you are sailing from Trinidad you will almost certainly have to motor sail hard on the wind so as not to be swept back to Crown Point.

If you are coming from Crown Point, stay well clear of the coastline to Lowlands Point. In addition, whichever way you come, be very careful to avoid the Bulldog Shoal.

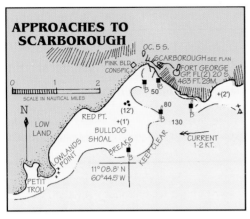

APPROACHES TO SCARBOROUGH

OC. 5 S.
SCARBOROUGH SEE PLAN
PINK BLD CONSPIC.
FORT GEORGE
GP. FL (2) 20 S.
463 FT. 29 M.
SCALE IN NAUTICAL MILES
N
RED PT.
LOW LAND
+(1')
(12')
BULLDOG SHOAL
LOWLANDS POINT
BREAKS
KEEP CLEAR
50
80
130
+(2')
CURRENT 1-2 KT.
11°08.8' N
60°44.5' W
PETIT TROU

Although Scarborough is well lit, the strong currents make it inadvisable to try entering after dark.

Regulations

Scarborough is a port of entry. Customs hours are Monday through Friday, from 0800-1600. Those clearing at other times will be charged overtime. As present regulations stand, you must sail your yacht to Scarborough to enter. You must visit customs which is upstairs in a red roofed building and then deal with immigration, on the third floor, in the NIB Mall which is across the street from the cruise ship dock.

This is clearly marked by a beacon. Stay well outside this beacon and continue to the entrance beacons. You have to allow for the current which sweeps you into the shallow water. Once you get past the entrance beacons head into town. You can anchor behind the new breakwater close to the Coast Guard dock. There are a few fingers at the base of this dock that you can tie up to while you clear customs and immigration. Do not anchor too close to the customs dock as the ferry from Trinidad does on occasion use it and needs plenty of room to maneuver. The alternative is to anchor outside the breakwater which is most uncomfortable in anything but the calmest weather.

Services

Yachting is not yet big enough in Tobago for many services to have developed. Water is available at the base of the cruise ship dock, on the west side. Check with the Port Authority first at the cruise ship terminal. This is not a dock designed for yachts and therefore high off the water. Unless you are going to take on a large amount, it may be easier to jerry jug it as you would the fuel from any of the nearby gas stations, or from the Coast Guard dock.

On Carrington Street opposite customs there is a route taxi stand, you can use them to transport provisions and fuel or arrange

SCARBOROUGH

for a ride to other destinations. There is a laundromat at Shore Park, a short taxi ride from Scarborough. There are no chandleries as such but Tobago Hardware, near customs and Sanka's Hardware on Sangster Hill Road are both general hardware stores. Close by is Sangster Hill Mall where there is a fishing supply store, an electrical store and the TIDCO office, who can be of help with information. Ice is available from the supermarkets and gas stations.

Ashore

The current supermarkets in Scarborough are not new and gleaming, but they are well stocked with essentials. Maharaj Supermarket is on the corner of Main and Burnett Streets and View Port is past customs just before the mall. The produce market behind the NIB Mall is large with many fruits, vegetables and fish. There are banks all over town and the NIB Mall has a travel agent and a variety of shops as well as the Tourist office on the third floor.

Stechers on Northside Road has mainly jewelry, watches and quality ornaments. It is also worth checking out the local vendors market on Carrington Street. The Cotton House is a batik studio just past the Old Donkey Cart House on Bacolet Street, where fabrics are hand waxed, painted, dyed and made into comfortable garments. They are open everyday of the week half day on Saturday, you may want to take a cab here as it is a good 15 minute walk from town. It is also worth checking out the local vendors market on Carrington Street.

Scarborough has many cheap and cheerful bars and restaurants and loud music is often dished in such generous amounts that it is like eating in a discotheque. This can be fun, the prices are unbeatable, and the food is very local.

For the older at heart there are three excellent restaurants where the fare is first rate and the ambience delightful. Rouselle's (B-C), owned by Bobbie Evans, is a 5-minute walk down Bacolet Street. It is upstairs and has a light airy feel. You can eat out on the balcony, or just while away some time at the bar looking out over the

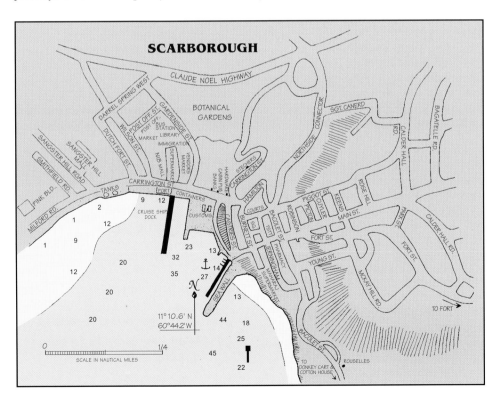

BURNETT STREET, SCARBOROUGH

sea. They offer a choice of full dinners which always include delicious soups and fresh local seafood, cooked to perfection. Lobster is often available. Open from 1500 to 2300, Monday to Saturday, it is advisable to book in advance.

The Old Donkey Cart House (B-D) is a 10-minute walk beyond Rouselle's on Bacolet Street. It is set in a traditional plantation house which is over 100 years old. You sit and eat in the pleasant garden surrounded by flowers. Kenny will proudly present the a la carte menu which is about the largest in Tobago, with a choice of anything from lobster to pasta.

The Blue Crab (B-C) is right in town on Robinson Street. It has a view over town to the bay. They are open for lunch and dinner everyday except Thursdays and Sundays. Expect good local food. Seafood is always available.

King's Well Inn (D) on the corner of Carrington and Burnette is owned and run by Kim and Cheryl. They serve local food in a roofed terrace open to the breeze.

The hilly part of Scarborough is capped by the ruins of Fort King George which is set in an immaculately kept garden of flowering trees and shrubs. Nearly a dozen huge old saman trees add class, as well as shade and support generations of epiphytes. The combination of the tended gardens and the magnificent views makes this a perfect place to relax. As for the rest, Some buildings are in good repair, but the hurricane of 1847 blew the roofs off many structures. On the grounds is a local art gallery and The Tobago Museum at the fort is open from Monday to Friday from 0900 to 1630. There is a small admission fee ($3TT adult, $1TT child).

There is also a botanical garden in town. Some areas of the garden are quite pleasant, though overall they are not as attractive as the fort.

Scarborough is the home of Kalina Cats a charter company that offers day sails around Tobago as well as inter-island cruises.

CROWN POINT TO PIGEON POINT

The western side of Tobago is low lying, with picture perfect white sand beaches separated by rocky outcroppings. Much of the hotel activity on Tobago is concentrated in this small area which is also near the airport.

Navigation

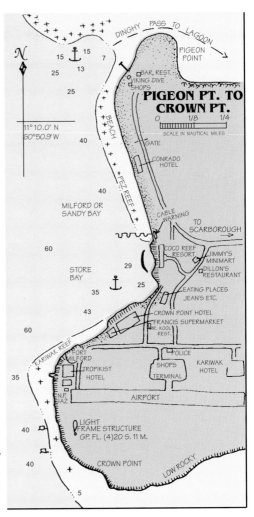

If you are arriving from the north, stay well clear of Buccoo Reef to the north. If you are sailing from Scarborough, stay well clear of the shallow water on the western end of the south coast.

The main anchorage is in Store Bay and this is well protected except in times of northerly swells. Do not anchor opposite the cable warning sign on shore.

An alternative anchorage is off Pigeon Point about a mile farther north. Eyeball your way in, favoring the Buccoo Reef side. Anchor just south of the reef in about 15-18 feet of water. Try to choose a patch of sand as there are a few soft and hard corals which could be harmed, especially in the shallower depths. This anchorage is beautiful with the reef on one side and Pigeon Point on the other. It can roll somewhat, especially at high tide. There is also a dinghy passage around Pigeon Point into Bon Accord Lagoon. It should be noted that Pigeon Point beach is the only privately owned beach in Tobago. This anchorage is part of the Bucco Reef Restricted area and sometimes they allow yachts here and sometimes they do not. They look more favorably on those with holding tanks.

Services

Pigeon Point Resort (VHF:06) requires you register with them if you anchor off their beach. The office is upstairs of the restaurant. TT$ 50.00 per boat per week allows full use of the facilities, for those not wanting the weekly rate the charge will be TT$ 10.00 per person per day. the facilities include: toilets, showers, garbage disposal, dinghy dock (tie on the shore side of the T on either side) and car parking. Ice and water are available as well as fax, message and taxi service.

The restaurant and bar are open daily.

Pets are not allowed on the premises. Pigeon Point had changed hands while we were going to press and a large resort was planned in this area.

Goran at Viking Dive (VHF:71) has a dive shop close to the dock and will send faxes, help arrange shopping, propane, gas and try to sort out any problem you may have.

Ashore

The intrepid shopper should pay a visit to The Young King of the Island Craft Shop that features work by Superfly, a versatile craftsman who works with coral, wood,

STORE BAY

leather and cloth, and is open everyday from 1000 to 1700. The Pigeon Point Boutique, run by Erika Hawkins, has a good selection of beachware, jewelry, books and gifts and is also open everyday 1000 to 1700.

Down the road towards Crown Point, Shore Things at the Conrado Hotel has good quality clothes and gifts. Take a break from shopping in their bar and restaurant. T-shirt and fabric vendors brighten up the roadside along the beach.

In Crown Point a lazy holiday attitude is widespread and there are plenty of shops and restaurants. If you have too much energy to lime, you can rent a bike at the roadside and work it off. You can also rent cars or scooters from some hotels or at the airport.

You can top up on provisions and get your bus tickets at Jimmie's Mini Mart on the main road open everyday from 0700 to 2300 or Francis Supermarket at the Crown Point Beach Hotel. They are open everyday except Sundays, 0800 to 1800, and have some pharmaceutical items as well as a good selection of basics. Francis Supermarket sells ice and stocks beer and soda in cans, rather than bottles, especially for people on boats. Good fresh vegetables are available

from a truck which parks just outside every day. There are food carts along the roads.

There are two bigger supermarkets. Penny Savers and View Port, about a mile down the main road towards Scarborough.

There are banks at the airport and the boutiques there include Christie's for t-shirts and film, The News stand for books, Karri for a wide range of handicrafts, including leatherwork, batik, pottery and carvings, and Native Instincts for gifts. All accept credit cards. Most of the larger hotels have small shops. For cooking gaz, go to NP at the west end of the airstrip.

The restaurants range from local small buildings on the beach to more elegant hotel verandahs. Close to the beach at Store Bay Miss Jean's Local Dishes is the first of a series of small restaurants that serve big portions of down home food at very low prices. Sylvia, Esmie, Joicy and Alma each have restaurants in the same area. Mr Kool Restaurant (D) across from the side entrance to Crown Point Hotel opens for dinner every evening except Sundays and serves a wide selection of dishes in a semi-buffet style.

When you are ready for a bigger night out, the large hotels are happy to have guests. The newly opened Coco Reef Resort (A-B), the fancy red roofed structure to the north of the beach, has a breakwater and it's own beach which makes dinghy access easy, they have two restaurants and bars.

At the Tropikist Beach Hotel (B-C) the Poolside Bar and The Marina Restaurant serve breakfast lunch and dinner overlooking their swimming pool. For the best food try the Kariwak Village (B). It is back from the beach, but has a pleasant dining room and pool shaded by lush garden plants. They have a set four course dinner with a choice of main courses and fresh seafood is always available.

The Bay Restaurant (C) at the Crown Point Hotel is arranged around a pool with a view of the bay. They are open every night, or try the Conrado Beach Hotel, out toward Pigeon Point and right on the beach.

While you are walking around, look at the remains of Fort Milford just past the Crown Point Hotel. These ruins are in a tidy small park overlooking both Store Bay and Milford Bay. Benches under the almond trees offer yet another shady spot to sit and relax. This fort was built by the British in 1777. It was built on the site of an early Dutch redoubt which occupied the site from 1642 to 1660.

Water Sports

Buccoo Reef is great for snorkeling, and one of the advantages of the Pigeon Point anchorage is that you are within swimming distance of the reef. It should be noted that this whole area is a national park and fishing or collecting shells or corals is forbidden.

The western end of Tobago is a popular area for diving. However, as the currents can be strong, many dives are done as drift dives and are best done with the local dive shop. One dive, called Flying Reef, is off the southwest coast. This is an undulating reef at 60 feet with plenty of hard and soft corals. You are likely to see turtles, sting rays, eels, lobsters, barracudas, and nurse sharks. The Shallows (on Drew Shoal) is an advanced drift dive in up to 90 feet. You dive over a coral bank richly textured with drop offs and changing contours. You are likely to see black-tipped sharks, hammerhead sharks, barracudas, turtles, groupers and sting rays. Mt. Irvine Wall off Mt. Irvine Bay is a wall dropping to about 60 feet. There are amazing underwater caves and tunnels that you can swim through and you will see lots of lobsters, eels, and a variety of reef fish including snappers and groupers.

Goran who runs the Viking Dive Shop (VHF:71) is a yachtsperson who has sailed all over the Caribbean and he will go out of his way to help people on yachts. You will normally find him at his Pigeon Point dive shop, though he also keeps another facility opposite the Crown Point Hotel. All kinds of courses and dives can be arranged, and he will be happy to pick you up from your yacht. He also takes divers to the eastern part of the island.

BUCCOO REEF AND BON ACCORD LAGOON

Regulations

Buccoo reef is one of Tobago's national parks. All the marine life is protected and fishing is not allowed, nor is removing or harming corals, shells or other sealife, anchoring your yacht here is not allowed. Buccoo Reef offers miles of good snorkeling with lots of fish and it is easily explored by dinghy. You should be very careful when you anchor your dinghy not to damage any coral. Watch out for the current.

Bon Accord Lagoon, also a national park, is the most protected anchorage in Tobago but is also restricted and can only be used in the case of a hurricane. The beach on No Man's Land is quite delightful and very popular for daytime picnics on weekends. Both No Man's Land and the lagoon are easily accessible by dinghy from Pigeon Point or Store Bay.

Navigation

This is all a restricted area, we only give navigation instructions in case you need to

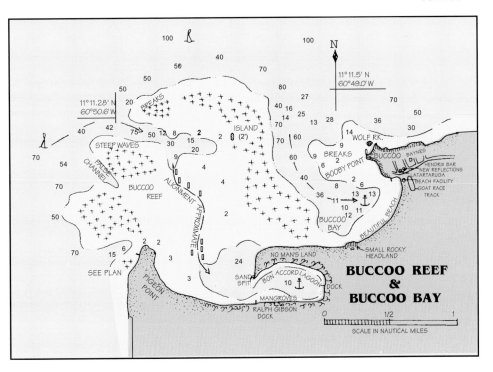

BUCCOO REEF
&
BUCCOO BAY

SCALE IN NAUTICAL MILES

shelter from a hurricane.

Finding your way into the deep area inside Buccoo Reef is no problem. Approach from the south when the light is good and follow the outer reef, keeping a safe distance off. The false channel is quite narrow and easy to identify. The next channel is the real one. If visibility is not good, go to the southern of the two large reef marker buoys. Head slightly to the right of the next (northeastern) marker buoy. Before long you will see breaking water ahead of you on the north side of the entrance channel. After that, eyeball your way in.

The channel into the lagoon is a little less than four feet at low water and about six to seven feet at high water. This is a comfortable channel for yachts drawing up to five feet and a possible channel for boats with six foot draft. While slightly deeper draft boats can make it in, it does not leave any room for error. Since there is lots of coral

and some swell, the entrance should not be undertaken lightly. Unless you know the area well, go in on a rising tide.

The long windy channel into the lagoon is marked by green stakes (mainly iron pipes with sticks in them) which you leave close on your port side. There is also one obvious starboard stake right near the end, pass outside the murky colored water marking the sand spit, but do not go too far over toward the other side as that, too, is shoal. Inside the lagoon there is a vast anchoring area, with about 10 feet of water.

Ashore

Bon Accord Lagoon is a large mangrove area, and quite a few birds use the mangroves for roosting at night. There are two small docks where you can get ashore. The Ralph Gibson dock allows you access to the road. Tie your dinghy up in the mangrove trees so you won't be in anyone's way.

BUCCOO BAY

Buccoo Bay is a pleasant, quite well protected anchorage and on most days of the week Buccoo is a peaceful waterside village. This all changes on a Sunday night at 2200 when they have what is known as Sunday School. People come from all over the island for an all night fete of drinking, merry making and music so powerful you can hear it to Pigeon Point. Drinks and food are available all evening long to keep you going. Buccoo village also hosts another famous national event, an annual goat race, which takes place on the Tuesday following Easter Monday.

Regulations

Buccoo Bay may soon be part of the Buccoo Reef National Park. In this case anchoring may be restricted here.

Navigation

The approach to Buccoo is not quite as bad as it looks on the charts, but you should approach in sunlight when you can see the shoals. You would not want to enter in large swells. More people seem to run aground here than elsewhere so if you are not a first rate reef navigator, give it a miss.

If you are coming from the west, pass outside Buccoo Reef, staying outside the buoys.

A good place to start your approach is outside Buccoo Reef on the eastern side opposite the small sand island. Head for the rocky area that interrupts the beach. You can keep track of your position by noting when the low island lines up with Pigeon Point and later when Rocky Point and Booby Point line up. (See also Mt. Irvine Bay sketch chart.)

Try to eyeball your way past the 14-foot patch. If you find yourself in it, it is probably best to edge back out into deeper water. Look for the 2-foot patch which breaks even in moderate seas. Eyeball your way past

this, staying over on the reef side of the channel in water 30 to 50 feet deep. As you get past the shoal area, ease around and head toward the village, passing over water that is mainly 11 to 13 feet deep. Anchor in about 13 feet between Booby Point and the small rocky outcropping on the beach opposite.

Ashore

There is a good little wall and dock for leaving your dinghy, but you will need a stern anchor.

Buccoo has a gorgeous beach and there are several boatmen here who make their living taking people out to Buccoo Reef or arranging picnics on No Man's Land.

There are a couple of good restaurants. Baynes Seafood House (B-C) opens every day except Thursday 1200-2300 from November to February and 1500-2300 from March to October. They serve a wide variety of seafood dishes.

La Tartaruga (C closed Sunday and Monday) is in a pleasant modern building right by the dock. It opens for dinner only and serves good Italian food.

Right next to La Tartaruga is the New Reflections, a boutique with an unusual but attractive loose pebble floor that sells all locally made items of clothing, arts and crafts. Open Monday to Saturday from 0900 to 2100, and on Sunday from 1900 to Midnight.

There are also a few local bars such as Hendrix Hideaway which sometimes serve food.

Esse's, just down the road on the right, is a small mini market and general store.

MOUNT IRVINE BAY

This is a prosperous and attractive resort area with a good public beach. The anchorage inside Rocky Point is gorgeous with interesting rocks and a beach backed by a thicket of coconut palms and trees. You can scramble over the rocks to lovely small beaches on the point. The reef here is very good for snorkeling, with an abundance of sea life, both large and small. The Mount

Irvine Hotel which overlooks the bay is built on the site of a sugar plantation which was owned by Charles Irvine in the second half of the 18th century.

Navigation

The approach is easy. Anchor in the northeast corner off the bay, behind the local fishing boats, and well away from the reef.

Ashore

The public beach facility ashore, on the northern side, boasts the Waterfront Restaurant (C) open everyday 0730 to 2300 and operated by Mrs. Anderson, who currently holds the title of the best Bake & Fish in Trinidad & Tobago. She can also arrange to have your laundry done. The restaurant puts on a beach barbecue every Friday night. Next door the Ocean View Arts and Crafts Shop is a local cooperative which stocks locally made handicrafts, fabrics, t-shirts and a few jams and sauces. Mt. Irvine Watersports Centre has a phone that can be used for a small fee. The bus to Scarborough passes about every half hour. On the beach just south of this is a restaurant that is part of the Mt. Irvine Bay Hotel (C), open everyday 1000 to 1700. They do a barbecue on Sunday's.

Just down the road the Mt. Irvine Bay Hotel is one of Tobago's fanciest hotels and has the island's only golf course. For a fee you can enjoy this or play tennis. Equipment for both sports is available. The Mt. Irvine Bay Hotel also has elegant restaurants. The Sugar Mill (B) is built by the side of the pool with a panoramic view of the bay beside a well restored sugar mill that is over 200 years old. Le Beau Rivage (A), with a French trained chef, offers fancy cuisine, blending French know-how with local produce.

There is another local bar about a 10-minute walk in the direction of Plymouth, which sits atop a rocky hill overlooking the ocean. It is called appropriately enough the Ocean View Bar (D) open everyday, 0800 to 2200 serving drinks and local food prepared by Pearl Legerton. Across the road is Marie's Place open Monday-Saturday 0800 to 2000 and on Sunday 0900 to 1800. This is a new two storey structure with a restaurant on the top floor and a very well stocked market and boutique on the ground floor. Right next door to this is the Two Seasons Restaurant, (C-D) run by Sue and Dale, and open everyday for breakfast, lunch and dinner. They specialize in local food and pizza, as well as having fresh baked bread on sale. On Friday nights stalls set up to sell snacks on the little green opposite the Two Seasons from about 1800.

Also of interest in this area is the Grafton Caledonia Bird and Wildlife Sanctuary, accessible via a dirt road that branches off the main road. This used to be an estate, but when the nearby forest was wrecked by Hurricane Flora in 1963, birds sought food nearer to human habitation and the owners

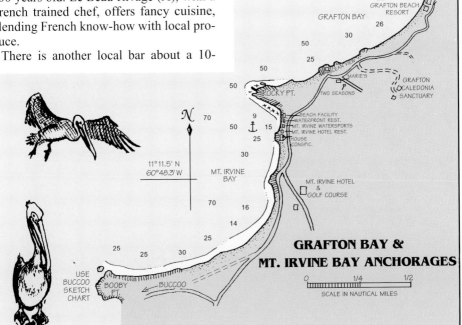

GRAFTON BAY & MT. IRVINE BAY ANCHORAGES

adopted these feathered orphans - feeding, watering and protecting them. Motmots are among the many colorful birds that can be seen on the nature trail. The best time to come for birdwatching is early morning or at sunset. There is no charge, but visitors are not allowed at night.

Water Sports

The Mt. Irvine Watersports Centre is right on the road and offers small sailing cats, windsurfing, waterskiing and diving. There is a reef in about nine feet of water off the rocks near the water sports centre which is worth checking out.

There are good dives along the coast. Arnos Vale Reef is an easy 30-foot dive, with lots of rocks encrusted with hard and soft corals and sponges with lots of reef fish. Englishman's Bay has rocks and walls dropping to 80 feet. These are well encrusted with marine life and support angelfish and parrotfish and turtles are sometimes seen.

GRAFTON BAY

Grafton Bay is used as one of the overnight anchorages during the annual Angostura Yachting World Regatta held in the early part of May. Although usually rolly, one can reduce this with the use of a second anchor to hold the bow or stern into the swell. the best place to anchor is close under the north point behind the fishing boats in about 30 ft. of water. Landing your dinghy on the beach can be a wet affair, it is best to do this right up on the north end of the beach.

Navigation

The approach is easy, The Grafton Beach Hotel and the larger pink Le Gran Courlan hotel beside it are easy to identify.

Ashore

The Grafton Beach Hotel has several shops selling crafts, gifts, books, film, clothes and pharmacy items. Cecily Gibbes in Kagm's sells clothes, bags and scarfs which she has designed and painted herself. There is also a beauty salon and car rental agency. Out on the point, what is left of Fort Bennett is surrounded by a little park with great views up and down the coast. A pleasant spot to sit for a while, doing very little. The upmarket Black Rock Cafe (A-B) is on the road towards Plymouth, and is open from 0730 to 2400 everyday and serves seafood and steak.

GREAT COURLAND BAY, BARREL OF BEEF IS VISIBLE IN THE FOREGROUND

BARREL OF BEEF

GREAT COURLAND BAY, PLYMOUTH

Plymouth is a delightful town set on a hill above a long pristine beach which is used by turtles to lay their eggs. One can sit for hours anchored close to Pelican Rock watching the antics of the seabirds. In the spring and summer when the laughing gulls are here, they badger the poor pelicans mercilessly, trying to steal the pelicans' fish by sitting on their heads and pecking at their bills. The pelicans have learned to keep their beaks underwater and spin in circles to get rid of the gulls before they lift their beaks to swallow their catch. We woke at dawn one morning to the sound of a heavy downpour. When we came on deck the source of the noise turned out to be tiny jumping fish that were so plentiful all the water in the bay was boiling. A flock of about a thousand seabirds, mainly gulls, pelicans and roseate terns crisscrossed the bay snatching at the fish and calling to each other.

Plymouth was the first English capital of Tobago and the site of a very early Dutch settlement in 1628. Later the Duke of Courland established a settlement here which was opportunistically taken over by the Dutch during a short interval when the Duke was imprisoned by the Swedes. When he was free the Duke got his godfather, Charles II of England, to give him a hand and the Dutch were expelled. After this the English kept a garrison of 50 men at the Courlander settlement but they were soon outwitted by the French. Twenty-five French soldiers sailed into Courland Bay at night, sneaked close to the fort and made an enormous racket the next morning, giving the

impression that there were hundreds of soldiers. The leader of the French force sought out the English commander and told him his position was hopeless as there were thousands of French soldiers poised to attack. The English commander, who had not yet had his first cup of tea, surrendered on the spot.

The indefatigable Duke of Courland claimed sovereignty again in 1682 in a joint venture with an Englishman, John Poyntz. Poyntz's role was to bring settlers and as part of his mission he wrote and published a description of Tobago that was so enticing that it is believed to have inspired Daniel Defoe to write Robinson Crusoe. Crusoe is quite a popular figure on Tobago. His cave has been identified, car rental agencies are

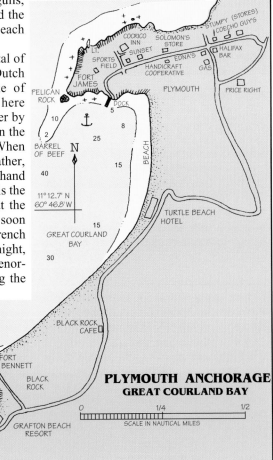

PLYMOUTH ANCHORAGE
GREAT COURLAND BAY

named in his honor and a dive shop commemorates Man Friday.

Both the ruins of Fort James, now surrounded by a well tended park, and a famous tombstone bring tourists to Plymouth. The large tombstone, for 23-year old Betty Stiven and her baby, dates from 1783 and states mysteriously that "she was a mother without knowing it, and a wife without letting her husband know it, except by her kind indulgence to him."

Navigation

About 200 yards southwest of Pelican Rock is a sunken rock, two feet underwater, called Barrel of Beef. It is part of a chain of rocks that extend from Pelican Rock. The rest of them are about 10 feet deep. Keep well clear of this area and approach Plymouth from the beach side.

Anchor off the dock in about 25 feet of water. Do not anchor off the Turtle Beach Hotel as this area is used by fishermen and you will be in the way.

If there is a surge, you may find you can make yourself more comfortable by using a stern anchor to keep your stern to the seas.

Ashore

There are several small supermarkets down the main road. If you want to do a large provisioning, it is only a short ride by bus, taxi or route taxi to Scarborough.

For lunch or an evening meal, you have a choice of the very local Sunset Restaurant, where you can eat well for a few dollars, or the Cocrico Inn will serve you a good local meal at a reasonable price. While you are here you can check out the small boutique which is open in the evenings. There are also plenty of local rum shops.

If you wander down to the Turtle Beach Hotel you will find a well stocked boutique and a choice of places to eat. The Kiskadee (B), has something special every night with entertainment that varies from a brass band, fire eating and limbo to folk dancing and a one man band. On different nights they have barbecues, buffets, set dinners and a la carte menus. There is also a coffee shop/beach bar where you can while away the hours, buy snack type meals, and listen to a steel band, (usually Saturdays). Tuesdays at 1730 David Rooks gives a nature talk on the various tours available in Tobago, including the rainforest and Little Tobago.

Just north of Plymouth is Adventure Farm, open everyday except Saturdays. It is a 12 acre estate that specializes in organic fruits. For about US$3 they will take you on a guided tour and point out the different trees, flowers and wildlife. Many of the trees and plants are labeled, and feeders scattered around bring the birds in close. Also available are refreshments and a variety of fresh fruits.

A little further along the same road is the romantic Arnos Vale Hotel (B) which is built out of an old plantation in a heavily forested hill which slopes to the sea. The restaurant is cool and breezy, in a large colonial room with antique furniture and a muralled wall. It overlooks the sea, and birdfeeders attract a large variety of birds. It is within walking distance of Plymouth and the snorkeling is good enough to be worth taking your gear over.

PLYMOUTH TO MAN OF WAR BAY

Once you have rounded Barrel of Beef in Plymouth, you can sail east along the shore all the way to Bloody Bay, and a quarter of a mile offshore clears all dangers. If the wind is east or south of east Tobago gives some protection from the seas and the sailing is usually very pleasant. After Bloody Bay you can pass between the Sisters and the Brothers. The two off-lying sunken Brothers are a danger, though you can often see one of them breaking. If you cannot see it, stay at least halfway over to the Sisters from the Brothers that you can see.

Between Plymouth and Man of War Bay there are several small anchorages. These can be wonderful calm overnight anchorages, or they can be so rolly it is impossible to land a dinghy on the shore. The only way to know is to go and look. If they are rolly, or conditions are not settled, it is better to consider them as daytime anchorages. We have not included Bloody Bay as this is poorly protected in most conditions.

BEACH AT GREAT COURLAND BAY

CASTARA BAY

Castara is a small fishing village set on a lovely beach with steep hills to the south.

Palace (D). Here you can get good rotis, chicken and chips, plus snacks.

Navigation

The approach is clear of shoals. If you are coming from or leaving to the east, pass outside the conspicuous White Rock.

The best protection is tucked right up in the northeast corner off the beach, but this area is used for seine netting, so it is better to anchor outside the fishing fleet in about 36 feet of water. Landing on the beach can be risky if there is a swell.

Ashore

There is a beach facility ashore. You can find a few essentials at Jackson's Grocery, Fellis Shop or the Vegetable Shop. There is a card phone opposite Fellis store. On the beach is the Cascreole restaurant where you can get inexpensive local food. If you walk up the hill on the road out of town heading east, you come to Ernest McKnight's Golden

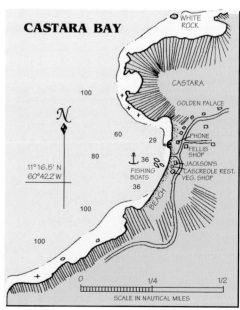

ENGLISHMAN'S BAY

ENGLISHMAN'S BAY

Scooped out of the rocky, forested coastline with a flawless golden beach at its head, Englishman's Bay makes a spectacular anchorage. The calmest and best spot is off the beach tucked up close to the eastern shore. Here you will find a large shelf of sand about 25 feet deep. If you see a small boat with a seine net anchored in the middle of the bay, be prepared to move while they fish. You will be out of their way tucked down in the southern part of the bay. Return when they have finished, because, should a swell come up in the night, the southern part of the bay could be very bad. If there are fishermen around and the southern part of the bay is too rolly to be tenable, carry on to Parlatuvier Bay or to Man of War Bay.

Ashore

Englishman's Bay is all part of Englishman's Bay Estate, which is a nature preserve and a low key development for nature lovers. The scenery here is gorgeous, so walks in any direction, on or off the road, are rewarding. There is a picknicking and barbecuing facility at the western end of the beach which you are welcome to use.

Water Sports

The snorkeling along the rocky eastern side of the bay is good, there are walls dropping to 80 feet. These are well encrusted with marine life and support angelfish, parrotfish and all the usual reef fish. In addition you are likely to see turtles. If there is any swell running though, the water may be murky.

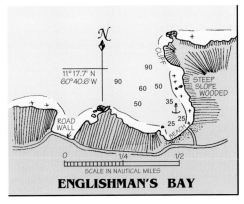

ENGLISHMAN'S BAY

111

PARLATUVIER BAY

The northeast coast gets progressively higher, steeper and more wild as you sail from west to east. The black rocks that edge the sea give way to a band of light colored grasses in the dry season. Above are vivid green shrubs, dull yellow bamboos and big patches of waving balisiers. Interspersed among these you will see the glint of silver thatch palms.

Parlatuvier Bay is considerably more protected than the previous anchorages and it, too, is very picturesque with a long white sand beach and a small fishing village. There is a long and high concrete dock on the north side of the bay. Water is available there and a lower section of the dock can be used to tie up your dinghy.

Anchor off the fishing fleet in about 40 feet of water. It is unwise to anchor in the south side of the bay as it is used for seine netting.

Ashore

You can buy essentials at the Chance Variety Store. Mr. and Mrs. Chance also run a guest house and are happy to see visitors. There is a card phone opposite

their shop. A little ways up the road and sitting high up on stilts, is the Riverside Restaurant (C-D) open everyday for lunch and dinner.

If you follow the road that leads off the dock, cross the main road and follow the river up through the bamboo stands, you will shortly come to a lovely little waterfall. Otherwise there is not much to do except watch the fishermen, laze on the beach or hike up the hills for a birds eye view of the coast.

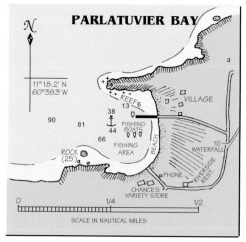

MAN OF WAR BAY AND CHARLOTTEVILLE

Man of War Bay is a spectacularly beautiful natural harbor. Nearly two miles wide and a mile deep, it is surrounded by steep convoluted hills of tropical forest with many small valleys and dainty beaches. If you are lucky enough to come when the hills are lit by glowing yellow trees during the dry season, you may have trouble putting your camera down.

Charlotteville is a pleasant sleepy town on a long beach in Man of War Bay's south-

eastern corner. Until the 1930's when a decent road was built, most of Charlotteville's business was conducted by sea. It was a thriving agricultural area and by 1865 the several estates which farmed the region were joined into a 11,000-acre holding owned by the Turpin family. As in many other parts of the Caribbean, diverse plantings were all given over to sugar cane production in the early years of slavery. Cotton, cocoa and bananas have since risen

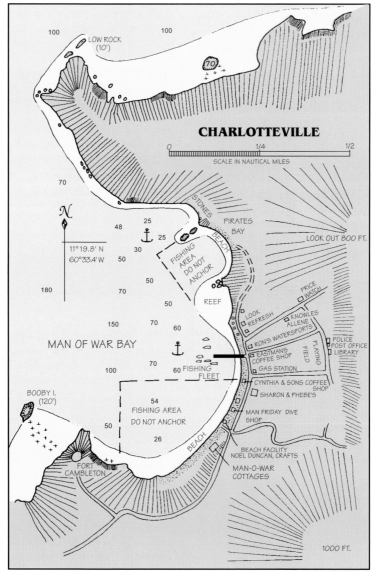

and fallen in prominence.

Fish production in the bay has always been good and a fishing cooperative has been set up to market the catch, which comprises about half Tobago's total. Much of the fishing is done by seine net. Spotters on the hills look for arriving shoals of fish and direct the fishermen below to encircle them. On a bountiful day hundreds of good sized fish are netted.

Navigation

Avoid the western side of Man of War Bay which is rough and has at least one sunken rock. The eastern side of the bay is well protected, though it would be uncomfortable in a northerly swell. Since fishing is vitally important you cannot anchor off the beach areas where seine netting is done, and this leaves two good anchorages.

The best anchorage is outside the fishing fleet, anywhere north of the gas station. The holding is good, but it is 60 to 70 feet deep so you will need lots of anchor line. You can also find good anchorage in Pirates Bay to the north, off the outcropping rocks. Here the water is only 25-30 feet deep, but this would be a totally untenable anchorage should a northerly swell come up.

Make sure you are anchored well clear of any reefs including the one that extends to sea between town and Pirate's Bay.

Services

You can jerry jug diesel, gasoline and kerosene from the gas station which also sells ice. The dock has a small, low section on the north side where you can tie up your dinghy.

Ashore

Charlotteville is a sleepy seaside village where no one is in a hurry and it is easy to make friends.

A few essentials can be found in the small shops in town, and people sometimes sell fruit and vegetables from the roadside. Eileen Murray at Local Refresh sells fresh homemade bread. Anytime you hear the sound of a conch shell, come in to buy fresh fish.

Route taxis leave for Scarborough in the mornings so you can always go to town to shop.

Should your stocks run low, do not worry. There are a couple of good, inexpensive restaurant ashore where you can eat tasty local food. Sharon and Phebe's (D) is the prettiest and has the most pleasant ambiance, with neat table cloths and a lovely view of the bay below. They are open everyday from 0800 onwards, have a happy hour on Fridays from 1700-1800. They can also arrange for laundry and tours to Argyle and Goldsborough waterfalls. When you want a change, Eastman's (D) offers light local snacks.

Those who would like to find some unusual souvenirs should wander down to the beach facility where Noel Duncan, a real artist, does wonders with calabash, leather and seeds.

On the far side of the playing field next to the police station and post office is a large, modern and air-conditioned library. Here you can sit and cool out for a few hours and enjoy a wide variety of reading material.

And for the music minded, Vanley Perry, who lived in Trinidad for 17 years and made pans (steel drums) for such famous groups as Angel Harps, Silver Stars and the Blue Diamonds, will be happy to demonstrate how pans are made and played. He can be contacted by calling Mr. Carrington at 660-4409. Vanley leads a steel band group called The Perry Kids who play at Sharon and Phebe's and Blue Waters Inn.

I can think of nowhere in the Caribbean where such beautiful walks are so easily available. The easiest is the path over the hill to Pirates Bay. The hillsides are a wild garden of balisiers and tropical trees with precipitous views of the reefs, beaches and sea. In the other direction the hike up to Fort Cambelton will reward you with photogenic vistas of the bay. Visit the Lookout as well, take any transport as far as the Lookout road, hike up to the Lookout. Apart from the panorama you will see anis, motmots, yellow tails, tanagers and parrots.

Serious hikers should go and chat with Pat Turpin of Pioneer Journeys at Man O'War Cottages. She keeps the local hiking guide as well as other nature books in stock and can point you in the right direction. Pat also organizes first rate nature tours.

CHARLOTTEVILLE

Water Sports

This is another excellent area of Tobago for diving. There are many sites with miles of underwater rocks and reefs. Since the current can occasionally be strong, most dives are done as drift dives. One of the many sites is St. Giles Island, a vast area of reefs and rocks from 20 to 60 feet deep. Huge building-sized rocks provide walls, crevices and caves which keep turning up unexpected surprises - a six-foot nurse shark complete with three remoras, sleeping in a cavern; a broad passageway where half a dozen giant-sized queen and French angel-fish swim up as if to say hello; a huge tarpon disappearing into the distance. The massive brain corals are impressive as are the colors of the sponges, which glow brightly in shades of green and blue.

There are two local dive operations, Ron's Watersports, run by Ronald Tiah is located directly across from the dock and is well recommended. Man Friday Diving is located a little further south down the beach, and is run in a pleasantly laid back manner by Bjarne from Denmark. Wander over and chat with them. They will be happy to pick you up from your yacht.

115

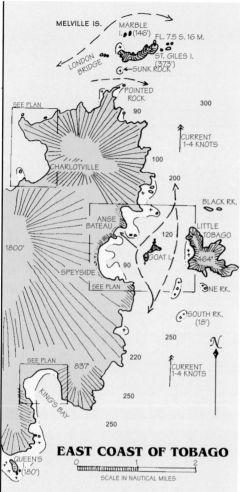

EAST COAST OF TOBAGO

SCALE IN NAUTICAL MILES

the passage between Speyside and Little Tobago can be very pleasant. The east coast also has one of Tobago's nicest little anchorages; Anse Bateau.

There is a little group of islands off the northeast tip of Tobago. London Bridge is the one with the dramatic hole going all the way through. The Melville Islands are a little farther along. They include the 72-acre St. Giles Island and were given to the government in 1968 by Charles Turpin as a nature preserve. Frigatebirds, boobies and many other seabirds nest here, and you cannot land without permission from the wildlife warden.

Navigation

The southwesterly equatorial current hits Tobago and divides, pushing westwards down the south coast and northwards along the East Coast. This northerly current is usually at its worst on the eastern side of little Tobago, so it pays to pass between Little Tobago and Speyside. The current is affected by the state of the tide. It is generally strengthened on the falling tide and weakened on a rising tide. At full or new moon, when tides are higher, their effect on the current is stronger. On a falling tide around new or full moon you can get up to four or five knots sweeping up inside Little Tobago. At other times you can get as little as one knot.

The first decision is whether to go inside or outside London Bridge and the Melville Islands. Outside is safer and easier, but it takes you farther north, and out into stronger current. It is the only way to go if you plan to sail, or have any doubts about the inside passage. If you have a reasonable motor, the inside passage can save time. There is plenty of water between St. Giles Islands and Pointed Rock, but the presence of a nasty sunken rock in the middle of the fairly narrow channel makes it challenging. I would only attempt this passage in reasonably calm conditions. If you can see breaking water on the sunken rock, going inside is no problem. Even if you cannot see it, you should be OK if you stay close to the northern coast of Tobago and then when

Much of the coast at the eastern end of Tobago rises steeply from the sea. These inaccessible cliffs and the many offshore islands provide safe nesting areas for seabirds, whose on-the-ground nests are easy prey for many mammals. The nearby seapermarket is exceptionally well-stocked because Tobago lies at the edge of a continental shelf and an upwelling of deep water brings nutrient concentrate from the sea bed. The result is an abundance of frigatebirds, laughing gulls, boobies, terns and tropicbirds.

The east coast of Tobago can be rough if the wind is strong and the current is ripping through. On the other hand, on a calm day, you get near Pointed Rock, pass it as closely as you safely can.

As you come down the east coast pass outside Long Rock, inside Little Tobago (sometimes called Bird of Paradise Island), either side of Goat Island, inside Middle Rock and South Rock.

Going north with the current behind you presents no problem. I would suggest passing outside the Melville Islands and London Bridge, admiring the scenery and the birds as you go.

ANSE BATEAU

Anse Bateau is a quite delightful anchorage and much calmer and more protected than one would expect looking at the charts. It is the only good anchorage on the east coast, and in the early days was used for careening sailing boats.

Anse Bateau is the home of Blue Waters Inn and it is set on its own amid steep wooded hills. There is a pristine beach with excellent snorkeling, diving and exploring. From the cockpit you can enjoy the views outwards toward Goat Island and Little Tobago.

Here you are close to all Tobago's major nature attractions, including the rain forest, the water falls and the Little Tobago bird sanctuary.

Navigation

You need to take care approaching and anchoring in Anse Bateau. There is an extensive reef off the southern headland. Most of the water over this reef is 12 feet deep, but there are a few six foot patches. Approach on a line between the house on Goat Island and the main building of Blue

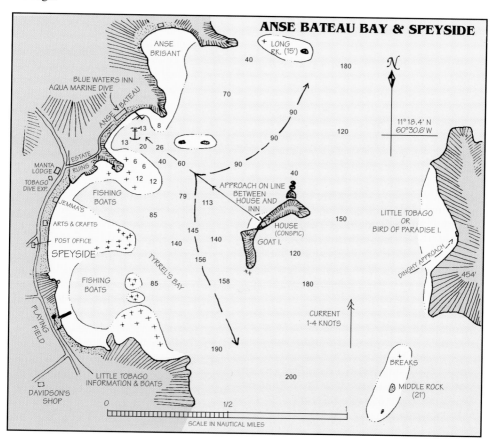

ANSE BATEAU BAY & SPEYSIDE

Waters Inn. Come in good light so you can see the shallow parts. The approach is over coral about 14-16 feet deep. Under no circumstances should you anchor on this coral which is easily damaged. Pass over it to the clear sand where you will find good anchorage in about 12-14 feet of water. There is only room for three or four boats here, so if it is crowded, consider returning another day.

Services

Reginald and Judy Maclean who manage the Blue Waters Inn (occasionally VHF:16) welcome yachts and have a few moorings available for TT$ 25.00 per night which they recommend you use rather than your anchor. Please register with them when you come ashore. Other facilities include water at their dock, a garbage service, toilet and shower facilities, full communications, and rental cars or taxis. They will try to help with ice. Keep in mind it is a low key, quiet establishment very much into ecotourism. Aqua Marine Dive Ltd is a full service dive center on the premises.

Ashore

If you run short of food you can try your luck in Speyside, at the Arts and Crafts Center (yes, it sells some food) or better yet at Davidson's Shop. You will enjoy the walk over the hill and through the old sugar mill ruins to Speyside. If you only end up with a bag of beans and a can of spam, don't despair, for you can always eat out. The Blue Waters Inn has a pleasant restaurant called The Fishpot overlooking the beach which opens from breakfast to dinner every day. Lunches are informal (D) and inexpensive. Dinners (B) are more elaborate and advance booking is requested. Seafood is always on the menu and you can often get lobster. The Shipwreck bar features local and Caribbean cocktails.

On the road to Speyside you will find the Manta Lodge whose aim is to encourage scuba divers, birdwatchers, artists and nature lovers. They have a boutique, dive shop, The Reef Bar and a restaurant (B).

A few other dive shops are to be found along the same road into Speyside.

In Speyside, Jemma's (C-D) is quite famous. You dine in a quaint tree house which is propped up on stilts around a large old almond tree hanging out to the surf line. A perfect atmosphere in which to enjoy her excellent Creole cooking, featuring chicken, fish, shrimp and lobster. Jemma opens for lunch and dinner, except on Fridays and Sundays when she closes at 1700 and Saturday when she is closed all day.

Dinghy exploration here is good, both around the islands and to Anse Brisant.

While you are anchored here a visit to Little Tobago Island should be on your agenda. You can do this by dinghy, or take one of the many little boats which ply the route. You can talk to Rennie right in Anse Bateau, or if you go to the dock in Speyside, you can talk to Terrence Gordon. Terrence is also willing to act as a guide to identify the birds while you are in Little Tobago. David Rooks also leads trips here on Thursdays.

Little Tobago is also known as Bird of Paradise Island because in 1909 its owner, wealthy British newspaperman William Ingram, imported 50 of these birds from their native New Guinea. At that time beautiful feathers were in high demand for ladies' hats and Ingram wanted to protect the Bird of Paradise from the hatters. The birds did well for many years and after Ingram's death his son deeded the island to the government with the stipulation that it be kept as a reserve. But Hurricane Flora, having no respect for deeds, blew almost all the elegant birds out to sea in 1963 and the few stragglers that survived soon died out. The government of New Guinea has offered to give Tobago some new birds, but local naturalists are of two minds about the proposal. Many native birds now thrive and breed on Little Tobago and might be displaced.

A trip to Little Tobago with a local guide will be the most rewarding way to see it, but even if you find your own way along the trail that goes up the hill from the small beach, you cannot miss getting good views of redbilled tropicbirds which are here during their nesting season from December to April. In season sooty terns, much prettier than their name suggests, brown noddies and

ANSE BATEAU

brown boobies can also be seen nesting on the rocks below the lookout. A forest ranger fills bamboo water troughs every day and these are used by many land birds. Blue-gray tanagers, white-tipped doves, Carib-bean elaenias, and bare-eyed thrushes come to drink while you are just a few feet away. Little bananaquits hop right in the drinking water for some vigorous bathing. Blue-crowned motmots are a common sight. Much

of Tobago's dry forest was destroyed by early planters, but on Little Tobago it was not cut because the island is too dry for farming. Beautiful white orchids, called virgin orchids, grow from many tree trunks.

Water Sports

The eastern end of Tobago has extensive reefs, clear water and spectacular diving and snorkeling. Occasionally the visibility drops for a few days because of currents coming up from the Orinoco River.

Keep in mind that currents are strong so dives are always drift dives. If you snorkel outside the protected bays, it is probably best to drift snorkel. Take your dinghy, and hang off it on a line. Let the current take you where it will and when you are done pop back in and hope the motor starts.

We will mention just a few of the many dives in this area. The Alps is out on the reef near Middle Rock. The dive starts in a most non-alpine way on a long flat area about 40 feet deep with all kinds of coral formations and small reef fish - a pleasant coral garden to get you really relaxed. Then there is a passage through a steep canyon in the rocks. On the far side the current sweeps you into a curious crater-like depression which forms an almost perfect circle - a kind of mini-amphitheater a couple of hundred feet across. Inside this area huge tarpon normally cruise, more curious than frightened by the divers. The crater was formed by the scouring action of breaking waves, and if you look above, they create a pattern of disturbed bubbles on the surface. On to the far side of the crater more large tarpon and pelagics roam, in addition to large and very tame angelfish.

Black Jack Hole is a dive in a large bay with about a 45-degree slope. The dive is normally done at 45 feet deep, though you can go down to 80 feet. There are two walls and an abundance of hard and soft corals. The dive got its name because towards the end of summer one can be greeted by the most amazing sight; the bay becomes alive with hundreds of large dark crevalle jacks. It is also just out of the fierce northerly current and this attracts big pelagics such as black-tipped sharks.

Coral Gardens is an easy and pleasant dive, amid a profusion of soft and hard corals, reef fish, banded coral shrimp and sponges. Tobago has some exceptional brain corals, but here is the largest of them all. Rising some eleven feet high and spreading sixteen feet in diameter, it is reputed to be the second largest in the world.

KING'S BAY

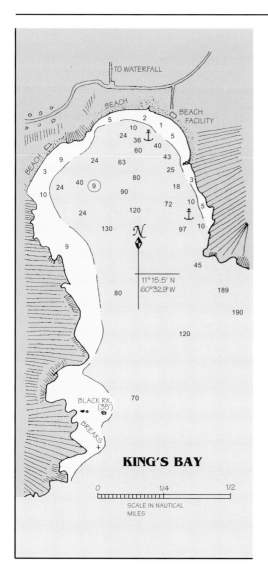

King's Bay is well protected, though you can get a swell in a southeasterly wind. The water in the bay is very deep and then shelves fast. If you don't have enough anchor line to be in the deep water, you can use two anchors, one in shallow water, and one out in deeper water to hold you in place. The best anchorage is off the eastern end of the beach in 40-60 feet. For more privacy you can anchor off the eastern shore a little to the south.

Ashore

Apart from the small beach facility there is not much ashore. While you are here you might take a walk to the King's Bay Waterfall. It is an attractive 20-minute walk, though the falls are a mere trickle if you go in the dry season. Land near the beach facility and follow the road back. Turn left at the main road and look for the waterfall sign on your right.

SOUTH COAST BETWEEN KING'S BAY AND SCARBOROUGH

There is no particularly good anchorage along this coast, so you might as well stay out in deep water and take advantage of the prevailing westerly current to sail down to Scarborough. Take care to stay outside the Great River Shoal as you approach Scarborough. Pass well outside Minster Rock which is buoyed.

121

With special thanks to Jody Feavearyear of the Strasenburgh Planetarium, Rochester, NY.

STAR

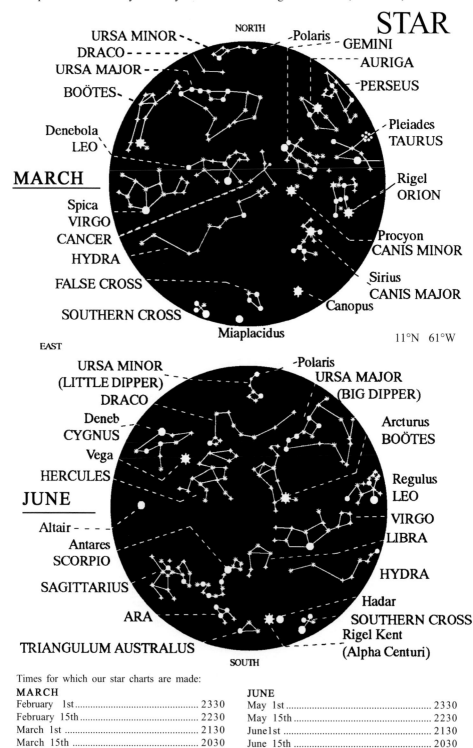

URSA MINOR
DRACO
URSA MAJOR
BOÖTES

NORTH
Polaris
GEMINI
AURIGA
PERSEUS

Denebola
LEO

Pleiades
TAURUS

MARCH

Rigel
ORION

Spica
VIRGO
CANCER
HYDRA
FALSE CROSS
SOUTHERN CROSS

Procyon
CANIS MINOR

Sirius
CANIS MAJOR

Canopus

Miaplacidus

11°N 61°W

EAST

URSA MINOR
(LITTLE DIPPER)
DRACO

Polaris
URSA MAJOR
(BIG DIPPER)

Deneb
CYGNUS
Vega
HERCULES

Arcturus
BOÖTES

Regulus
LEO

JUNE

VIRGO
LIBRA

Altair
Antares
SCORPIO
SAGITTARIUS
ARA
TRIANGULUM AUSTRALUS

HYDRA

Hadar
SOUTHERN CROSS
Rigel Kent
(Alpha Centuri)

SOUTH

Times for which our star charts are made:

MARCH		JUNE	
February 1st	2330	May 1st	2330
February 15th	2230	May 15th	2230
March 1st	2130	June 1st	2130
March 15th	2030	June 15th	2030
April 1st	1930	July 1st	1930
April 15th	1830	July 15th	1830

CHARTS

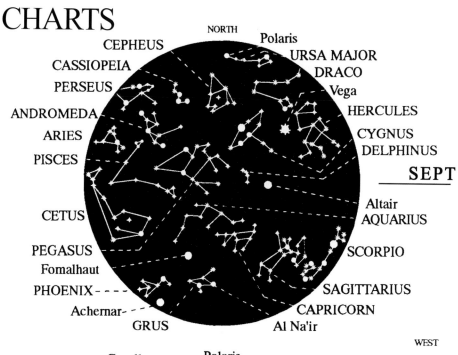

NORTH

CEPHEUS
Polaris
CASSIOPEIA
URSA MAJOR
PERSEUS
DRACO
Vega
ANDROMEDA
HERCULES
ARIES
CYGNUS
PISCES
DELPHINUS

SEPT

Altair
CETUS
AQUARIUS

PEGASUS
SCORPIO
Fomalhaut
PHOENIX
SAGITTARIUS
Achernar
CAPRICORN
GRUS
Al Na'ir

WEST

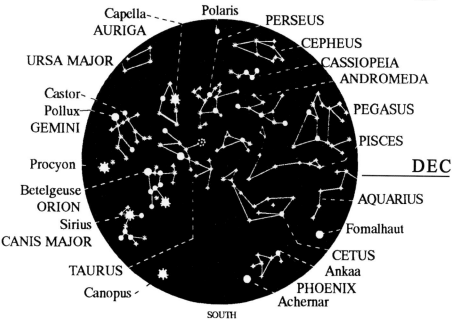

Capella
Polaris
AURIGA
PERSEUS
CEPHEUS
URSA MAJOR
CASSIOPEIA
ANDROMEDA
Castor
Pollux
PEGASUS
GEMINI
PISCES
Procyon

DEC

Betelgeuse
ORION
AQUARIUS
Sirius
CANIS MAJOR
Fomalhaut
TAURUS
CETUS
Ankaa
Canopus
PHOENIX
Achernar

SOUTH

DIRECTORY

This directory lists many of the services of interest to boaters in Trinidad and Tobago. Most entries have a page reference, This page reference refers to this guide and the reader can find further information by looking on the pages mentioned.

Those seeking information on services should also refer to our advertisers index. For information on other services you can consult the annual Boater's Directory

IMPORTANT NOTE:
To telephone Trinidad you currently dial 1-809 from most countries. This will be changing in June 1997 to 1-868

TRINIDAD

ABSENTEE YACHT CARE
Atlantic Yacht Services 634-4337 F:634-4437 VHF 68 e-mail:atlantic@trinidad.net
　　Page 61
CrewsInn 634-4384/5 F:634-4542 Page 61-62
IMS Yacht Services 625-2104/5 F:634-4437 VHF 68 e-mail: ims@tstt.net.tt Page 61
Peake Yacht Services Ltd. 634-4420/3/7 F:634-4387 VHF 69 Page 59-61
Power Boats Mutual Facilities Ltd. 634-4303 F:634-4327 VHF 72 Page 52-58
Trinidad & Tobago Yachting Association 634-4210 T/ F:634-4376 VHF 68, Page 68
Yacht Maintenance Services 633-7846, 634-4303, 634-4376 Page 63

ACCOMMODATIONS
Fantasy Island 622-6285 Page 66
Mt. Plasir Estate 670-8381 F:680-4553 Page 32
Peake Yacht Services Ltd. 634-4420/3/7 F:634-4387 VHF 69 Page 59-61
Power Boats Mutual Facilities Ltd. 634-4303 F:634-4327 VHF 72, Page 52-58
The Cove 634-4319 Page 65

ADHESIVES
3M Marine 623-8917 F:623-3079
Fortress Woodworking T/F:634-4510 VHF 72, Page 54, 56
Marc-One Marine Supplies 622-7926 F:622-1973, Page 64

BIMINIS & CANVAS
Barrow Sail Loft 632-4608 T/F:634-4137 VHF68 Page 58
Calypso Marine Canvas 633-8709, 634-4012, Page 61
Ocean Sails Ltd. 634-4560 F:634-4560, Page 61
Soca Sails 634-4384 ext 117 662-3377 #5467 Page 62
The Upholstery Shop 634-4143 VHF 72 Page 58
Webster's Marine Centre 625-8653

BOAT BUILDERS
Bowen Marine 634-4543, 634-4365 F:634-4228 Page 62

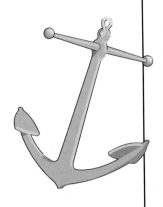

BOAT BUILDERS (CONT)
Calypso Marine Services 634-4551, 627-4550 VHF 68, Page 62
Formula III 634-4336 F:634-4009 VHF 68, Page 58
Kayak Centre 633-7871, 629-2680 Page 36
Peake Marine Limited 634-4423, 634-4427 F:634-4387 Page 59
Tropical Marine Ltd. 634-4502 F:634-4453 Page 63

CAR RENTALS
Convenient Rental Ltd. T/F:634-4017 VHF 68 Page 60
Mark's Rentals 632-8984, 625-8279 VHF 68 Page 58

CHANDLERIES
LP Marine & Industrial Supplies 633-3395 F:632-3441 e-mail: lpmarine@opus-networx.com, Page 73
Marine Hardware & Accessories 662-1781, 662-1782, 662-1783 Page 71-72
Peake Hardware 622-7325, 622-8816 F:622-7288 VHF 69 Page 70-71
Peake Yacht Services Ltd. 634-4420/3/7 F:634-4387 VHF 69 Page 59-61
The Boat Shop 634-2628 F:634-4148 VHF 72 Page 56, 72

CHARTER
Humingbird III, Stella Maris, T/F:634-4513 VHF 68 Page 62
Sail and Fly Travel Agency 634-4144 F:634-4392 VHF 68 e-mail: sailfly@trinidad.net
    Page 60
Tropical Air 622-4843 F:622-4843

CHARTS (see also chandleries)
Marine Consultants Ltd. 625-2887, 625-1309 F:625-2270 Page 75

COURIERS
DHL 625-9835
Federal Express 623-4070
UPS 624-4895

CUSTOMS
Customs 634-4341 Chaguaramas

DIVING
Dive Specialists Centre 634-4319 F:628-4524 VHF 68, Page 66

DIVING GEAR
Dive Specialists Centre 634-4319 F:628-4524 VHF 68, Page 66
The Boat Shop. 634-2628 F:634-4148 VHF 68,72 Page 56, 72

ELECTRICS

Caribbean Marine 634-4561 F:634-4561
  VHF 72, Page 56, 58
Dockyard Electrics 634-4933 F:634-4933
  VHF 68, Page 62
General Diesel Limited 657-6351, 652-
  5441 F:657-3927 Page 64
Lange Eighty 625-4825 F:653-3430, Page
  71
Marc-One Marine Supplies 622-7926
  F:622-1973, Page 64
Marine Electrical Systems 542-0802
  F:633-2580 Page 63
Serge's Electrical Workshop 634-4420 VHF69 Page 60

ELECTRONICS

Carlos Marine Electronics VHF 68, Page 61
LP Marine & Industrial Supplies 633-3395 F:632-3441 lpmarine@opus-networx.com
  Page 73
Max Serrao 622-1472 Page 71

FIBERGLASS REPAIR (see also haul-out)

Atlantic Yacht Services 634-4337 F:634-4437 VHF 68 e-mail: atlantic@trinidad.net
  Page 61
Awon's Marine Services 638-4505, 623-0859 F:637-6671 Page 63
Calypso Marine Services 634-4551, 627-4550 VHF 68 Page 62
Fiberglass Specialist-GYS 634-4303, 674-2402 Page 54
Formula III 634-4336 F:634-4009 VHF 68 Page 58
IMS Yacht Services 625-2104/5, 634-4328 F:634-4327 F:634-4329 VHF 68 e-mail:
  ims@tstt.net.tt Page 61
Rawle Walker 640-5048, 640-1982

FISHING

Alberts's Hardware 632-1023 Page 73
Calypso Marine Services 634-4551, 627-4550 VHF 68, Page 62
T&T Game Fishing Association 624-5304
The Tackle Shop 632-1782 F:632-1782 e-mail: tackle@trinidad.net Page 73

FUEL & WATER

CrewsInn 634-4384/5 F:634-4542, Page 61-62
Power Boats Mutual Facilities Ltd. 634-4303 F:634-4327 VHF 72
  Page 52-58
Trinidad & Tobago Yacht Club 633-7420 F:633-6388 Page 71

HARDWARE

Albert's Hardware 632-1023 Page 73
Marine Hardware & Accessories. 662-1781/2/3 Page 71-72

HARDWARE (CONT)
Peake Hardware 622-7325, 622-8816 F:622-7288 VHF 69 Page 70-71
Trestrails 623-6556 F:623-5319 Page 75
UAL Weldequip 663-9353 F:645-4887 Page 64
William H Scott Ltd. 623-2181/5 F:623-9346 Page 75

HAULOUT
CrewsInn 634-4384/5 F:634-4542 Page 61-62
IMS Yacht Services 625-2104/5 634-4328 F:634-4437 F:634-4329 VHF 68 e-mail:
    ims@tstt.net.tt Page 61
Peake Yacht Services Ltd. 634-4420/3/7 F:634-4387 VHF 69 Page 59-61
Power Boats Mutual Facilities Ltd. 634-4303 F:634-4327 VHF 72 Page 52-58
Trinidad & Tobago Yachting Association 634-4210, 634-4519 T/F:634-4376 VHF
    68 Page 67-69

IMMIGRATION
Immigration 634-4341, 623-8147

INFLATABLES
Marine Safety Equipment 634-4410 F:634-4410 Page 68
Power Boats - AB Inflatables 634-4303 F:634-4327 VHF 72 Page 52-58

INFORMATION
Local Operator/ Info. 6411
Overseas Operator 6211
TIDCO 624-2953, 624-0234, from USA:1-800-595-1868 Page 24
Tourism Office 623-6023
YSATT 634-4938, Page 24

INSULATION
Caribbean Insulation Services 659-2666, 659-3504   F:659-2687 e-mail:
    cisl@trinidad.net, Page 64

LAUNDRY
Chin's Laundry 622-3733, Page 68

MACHINING & FABRICATION
Ali's Machine Shop 634-4420, Page 60
Mark De Gannes 634-4025, Page 58
Propeller & Marine Service 634-4533 F:633-6294, Page 60

MARINA DOCKS
CrewsInn 634-4384/5 F:634-4542, Page 61-62
Fantasy Island 622-6285, Page 66
Peake Yacht Services Ltd. 634-4420/3/7 F:634-4387 VHF 69, Page 59-61

MARINA DOCKS (CONT)

Pier 1 634-4472, 634-4426 F:634-4556 e-mail: pier1@trinidad.net Page 67
Power Boats Mutual Facilities Ltd. 634-4303 F:634-4327 VHF 72 Page 52-58
Stella Maris 634-4513 F:634-4513 VHF 68 Page 62
Tardieu Marine Ltd. 634-4534 VHF 68 Page 63
Trinidad & Tobago Yacht Club 633-7420 F:633-6388 Page 70, 72
Trinidad & Tobago Yachting Association 634-4210 T/F:634-4376 VHF 68 Page 68
Tropical Marine Ltd. 634-4502 F:634-4453, Page 63

MECHANICS

Atlantic Yacht Services 634-4337 F:634-4437 VHF 68 e-mail: atlantic@trinidad.net, Page 61
Caribbean Marine 634-4561 F:634-4561 VHF 72, Page 56-58
General Diesel Limited 657-6351, 652-5441, F:657-3927, Page 64
Desi Macintosh Power Boats
Lawrence Placid Power Boats
LP Marine & Industrial Supplies 633-3395 F:632-3441 lpmarine@opus-networx.com, Page 73
Total Marine Services 634-4383 Page 58

MEDICAL

Community Hospital of Seventh Day Adventists 622-1191, 622-1192
Fire/ Ambulance 990
General Hospital 623-2951, 623-2952
Mount Hope Medical Sciences Complex 645-4673, 645-2640
St. Clair Medical Centre 628-1451, 628-1452

OPTICAL

Ferreira Optical Limited 623-4058 F:623-3473 Page, 75
Optometrists Today 624-3033 F:625-1914

OUTBOARDS

Bowen Marine Lt. 634-4543, 634-4365 F:634-4228 Page 62
Calypso Marine Services 634-4551 627-4550 VHF 68 61
Ian Keizer 634-4536
Peake Hardware 622-7325, 622-8816 F:622-7288 VHF 69 Page 70-71
Total Marine Services 634-4383 Page 58

PAINT APPLICATION

Awon's Marine Services 638-4505, 623-0859 F:637-6671 Page 63
Clyde Bernard (Teepo) Power Boats Page 63
CrewsInn 634-4384 F:634-4542 Page 61-62
Donald Carrington (Akee) 637-1182 Page 63
Formula III 634-4336 F:634-4009 VHF 68 Page 58
Fiberglass Specialist 634-4303, 674-2402 Page 58
IMS Yacht Services 625-2104/5, 634-4328 F:634-4327 F:634-4329 VHF 68 e-mail: ims@tstt.net.tt, Page 61

PAINT APPLICATION (CONT)

Peake Yacht Services 634-4387, 634-4423 F:634-4387 VHF 69 Page 59-61
Rawle Walker 640-5048, 640-1982
Yacht Maintenance Services 633-7846, 634-4303 634-4376 Page 63

PAINTS

IMS Yacht Services 625-2104/5, 634-4328 F:634-4327 F:634-4329 VHF 68 e-mail:
  ims@tstt.net.tt, Page 61
Marc-One Marine Supplies 622-7926 F:622-1973 Page 64

PARKS

Asa Wright 667-4655 Page 30-31
National Park Department 634-4349, 634-4227
Pointe-a-Pierre Wildfowl Trust 637-5154, 662-4040 Page 85
Timberline 638-2263 Page 31
WASA 622-2301/5 622-1965 Page 35

PETS

Dog House Pets & Supplies 652-4156, 628-2772 Page 20
Quarantine Guard 622-5986 Page 20
Veterinary Services 622-1221 Page 20

PHARMACIES

Glencoe Pharmacy 637-7565 Page 72

PHOTO

Avifauna Tours 633-5614 Page 34, 35
Dalla Costa's Film Processors 625-3907 Page 76

PROCUREMENT

Yachtfitters 638-4505 F:637-6671 VHF68 Page 63

PROVISIONING

Adam's Bagels 622-2435
  F:622-2435 Page 55
Hi-Lo Supermarket 633-0101
  VHF 72 Page 72
West Point Mini-Mart 634-
  4007 VHF 68 Page 60

REFRIGERATION
Daco Engineering Co. 637-3528 F:637-3528 Page 70

RESTAURANTS
Ali Baba Restaurant 622-5557 Page 79
Anchorage 634-4334 Page 69
Fantasy Island 622-6285 Page 66
Indigo 632-0451 Page 73
Jardin des Tuileries 632-0256 Page 73
La Boucan 624-3211 Page 78
Lifeline, Power Boats Page 65
Le Chateau De Poisson 622-6087 Page 78-79
Lychee Garden 637-2668 Page 73
Monsoon 628-7684 Page 78
Moon Over Bourbon Street 637-3448 Page 73
Nip'N' Tuck 634-4438 Page 65
Panda Palace 622-4462 Page 78
Phyllis Viera's Verandah 622-6287 Page 76
Pier 1 634-4472 634-4426 F:634-4556 e-mail: pier1@trinidad.net Page 67
Pisces on the Sea 637-8486 Page 72
Pizza-Burger Boys 633-2697 Page 72-73
Rafters 628-9258 Page 77
Seabelle 622-3594 Page 73

RESTAURANTS (CONT)
The Bight 634-4423 Page 65
The Lighthouse Grub and Grog 634-4384 F:634-4542 Page 15, 65
The Pelican Inn Pub 624-7486 Page 77
Tiki Village 622-6441 Page 76
Timberline resort 638-2263 Page 31, 86
Trinidad & Tobago Yachting Association 634-4210 T/F:634-4376 VHF 68 Page 68
Wok 'n Roll 633-7655 Page 73
Woodford Cafe 622-2233 Page 78

RIGGING
Ocean Sails Ltd. 634-4560 F:634-4560 Page 61
Peake Yacht Services Ltd. 634-4420/3/7 F:634-4387 VHF 69 Page 59-61

SAFETY EQUIPMENT
Marine Consultants Ltd. 625-2887, 625-1309 F:625-2270, Page 75
Marine Safety Equipment 634-4410 F:634-4410, Page 68
UAL Weldequip 663-9353 F:645-4887 Page 64

SAILMAKERS
Barrow Sail Loft 632-4608 T/F:634-4137 VHF68 Page 58
Doyle Sails 632-0559 F: 632-0559, VHF 68, Page 64
Ocean Sails Ltd. 634-4560 F:634-4560, Page 61
Soca Sails 634-4384 ext.117, 662-3377 #5467 Page 59

SECURITY
Chaguaramas Security 634-4227
Coast Guard- Maritime Emergency 634-4440
Police 999

SHIPPING
Lazzari & Sampson Travel 623-2721/2/3/4 F:623-5776 VHF 68, Page 73, 75

SOLAR GENERATORS
Caribbean Marine 634-4561 F:634-4561 VHF 72, Page 56-58

SURVEYS
Bill Wray 634-4420, 634-4423 F:634-4387, Page 60

TAXIS
Ian VHF 68, Page 68
Junior 643-0397 VHF 68, Page 68
Sahden 662-5071
Victor 629-3488

TOURS
Avifauna Tours 633-5614 F:633-2580 Page 34-35
Chaguaramas Military History & Aviation Museum 634-4391 Page 69

TOURS (CONT)
Convenient Rental Ltd. 634-4017 F:634-4017 VHF 68 Page 36
Kayak Tours 629-2680 Page 30, 34, 36
Lazzari & Sampson Travel 623-2721/2/3/4 F:623-5776 VHF 68 Page 73, 75
Sail and Fly Travel Agency 634-4144 F:634-4392 VHF 68 e-mail sailfly@trinidad.net
     Page 32
Tours Incredible 624-0820 Page 72
Tropical Air 622-4843 F:622-4843
Winston Nanan's Tours 645-1305

TRAVEL
Lazzari & Sampson Travel 623-2721/2/3/4 F:623-5776 VHF 68 Page 73, 75
Sail and Fly Travel Agency 634-4144 F:634-4392 VHF 68 e-mail sailfly@trinidad.net
     Page 32

UPHOLSTERY
Calypso Marine Canvas 633-8709 634-4012 Page 61, 70
Lensyl Products Ltd. 662-7534 F:663-1454 Page 64
Radica Trading 627-2315 Page 75
The Upholstery Shop 634-4143 VHF 72 Page 58
Webster's Marine Centre 625-8653

WIND GENERATORS
Doug Bugger 634-4929 F:634-4387 VHF 72 Page 61

WOODWORKING
Atlantic Yacht Services 634-4337 F:634-4437 VHF 68 e-mail: atlantic@trinidad.net
     Page 61
Cask Woodworking 634-2275 VHF 69 Page 60
Fortress Woodworking 634-4510 F:634-4510 VHF 72 Page 54, 56
Shipshape Marine Services 650-1914 F:650-3688 Page 85
Shipwrights 634-4940 F:634-4939 e-mail shipwrights@Trinidad.net, Page 54

TOBAGO

ACCOMMODATIONS
Blue Waters Inn 660-4341, 660-4077 F:660-5195 e-mail: bwitobago@trinidad.net
   Page 118
Coco Reef Resort 639-8571 F:639-8574 Page 101
Lagoon Villas 639-8555
Man-O-War Bay Cottages 660-4327 F:660-4328 Page 114
Store Bay Holiday Resort 639-8810

CHARTERS
Kalina Cats 639-6304 F:639-6304 Page 98

COMMUNICATIONS
Blue Waters Inn 660-4341, 660-4077 F:660-5195 e-mail: bwitobago@trinidad.net
   Page 118
Mt. Irvine Watersports Centre 639-4008 T/F:639-9379 Page 105,106

COURIERS

Fed Ex 639-3450 Kandy Joseph

CUSTOMS
Customs 639-2415 Scarborough

DIVING
Aqua Marine Dive Ltd. 660-4341 F:639-4416 e-mail: bwitobago@trinidad.net,
   Page 118
Man Friday Diving 660-4676 F:660-4676 Page 115
Manta Lodge 660-5268 F:660-5030 Page 118
Mount Irvine Watersports Centre 639-4008 T/F: 639-9379 Page 105,106
Ron's Watersports 622-0459 F:673-0549 Page 115
Tobago Dive Experience 660-5268 F:660-5030 Page 118
Viking Dive Centre 639-9209 F:639-0414 Page 102

GOLF
Mt. Irvine Bay Hotel 639-8871, 639-8872 F:639-8800 Page 105

IMMIGRATION
Immigration 639-2931 Crown Point Airport

MEDICAL
Ambulance 639-2108
General Hospital 639-2551 Scarborough

PARKS
Adventure Farm Page 108
Grafton Caledonia Sanctuary Page 105
Little Tobago Page 118-120

PROVISIONS
Francis Supermarket 639-8440 Page 101
Jimmie's Mini Mart 639-8292 Page 101
Maharaj Supermarket Scarborough Page 97
Marie's Place 639-0859 Page 105
View Port Scarborough Page 97

RESTAURANTS
Arnos Vale Hotel 639-2881 F:639-4629 Page 108
Baynes Seafood House 639-9705 Page 104
Blue Crab Restaurant 639-2737 Page 98
Blue Waters Inn 660-4341 F:660-5195 e-mail: bwitobago@trinidad.net Page 118
Cascreole Page 110
Coco Reef Resort 639-8571 F:639-8574, Page 102
Cocrico Inn 639-2961 Page 108
Grafton Beach Resort 639-0191 Page 106
Hendrix Hideaway Page 104
Jemma's 660-4066 Page 118
Kariwak Village 639-8442 Page 102
King's Well Inn 639-3883 Page 98
KP's Patinos Buccoo 639-9481
La Tartaruga 639-9705 Page 104
Manta Lodge 660-5268 F:660-5030 Page 118
Marie's Place 639-0859` Page 105
McKnight's Golden Palace 639-5673 Page 110
Mr. Kool Restaurant 639-0025 Page 101
Mt. Irvine Bay Hotel 639-8871 639-8872 F:639-8800 Page 105
Ocean View Bar 639-0437 Page 105
Pigeon Point Resort 639-8141 F:639-7232 VHF 6 Page 99
Riverside Restaurant 639-5627 639-5628 Page 112
Rouselle's 639-4738 Page 97
Sharon & Phebe's Restaurant 660-5717 Page 114
The Bay Restaurant 639-8781 Page 102
The Black Rock Cafe 639-7625 Page 106
The Old Donkey Cart House 639-3551 Page 97
Tropikist Beach Hotel 639-8512 Page 102
Turtle Beach Hotel 639-2851, Page 107
Two Seasons Restaurant 639-9461, Page 105
Waterfront Restaurant 639-9613, Page, Page 105

SECURITY
Coast Guard 639-1461
Police 639-1200

SHOPS
New Reflections, Page 104
Pigeon Point Boutique 623-2454, Page 101
The Cotton House 639-2727 F:639-2727, Page 97

SHOPS (CONT)
Turtle Beach Hotel 639-2851, Page 108
Younk King of the Island Craft Shop, Page 99

TOURS
Blue Waters Inn 660-4341, F:660-5195 e-mail: bwitobago@trinidad.net, Page 118
David Rooks 639-4276 F:639-4276, Page 92
Pioneer Journeys 660-4327, 660-5175 F:660-4328, Page 92

WOODWORKING
Harmony Woodworking 639-5935 Arnos Vale Rd. Plymouth

EXTRA PHONE NUMBERS

NAME	NUMBER

GENERAL INDEX

See also our Directory Section which gives page number references for a large variety of headings including all yacht services.

NOTES

NOTES

NOTES

ADVERTISERS INDEX

CRUISING GUIDE PUBLICATIONS

ORDER FORM

To order, please fill out coupon on back and send check or money order to:
Cruising Guide Publications, P.O. Box 1017, Dunedin, Florida 34697-1017.
For credit card orders only, call 1-800-330-9542 • 1-888-330-9542
E-mail: (813-733-3565) -- cgp@earthlink.net

❑ $19.95   CRUISING GUIDE TO THE VIRGIN ISLANDS
(8th Edition) by Simon and Nancy Scott.

❑ $24.95   VIRGIN ANCHORAGES (New color aerial photos and color graphics)

❑ $19.95   CRUISING GUIDE TO THE LEEWARD ISLANDS--*With GPS
Coordinates* (4th Edition) by Chris Doyle.

❑ $19.95   SAILOR'S GUIDE TO THE WINDWARD ISLANDS
(8th Edition) by Chris Doyle.

❑ $24.95   CRUISING GUIDE TO TRINIDAD AND TOBAGO, VENEZUELA
AND BONAIRE (1st Edition) by Chris Doyle.

❑ $24.95   CRUISING GUIDE TO CUBA--*With GPS Coordinates and Charts*
(1st Edition) by Simon Charles.

❑ $24.95   GENTLEMAN'S GUIDE TO PASSAGES SOUTH--*5th Edition With GPS
Coordinates*--The "Thornless Path to Windward," by Bruce Van Sant.

❑ $15.95   CRUISING GUIDE TO THE SEA OF CORTEZ (From Mulege to La Paz)

❑ $14.95   CRUSING GUIDE TO TRINIDAD & TOBAGO by Chris Doyle.

❑ $19.95   CRUISING GUIDE TO THE FLORIDA KEYS by Capt. Frank Papy.

❑ $29.95   CRUISING GUIDE TO TAHITI AND THE FRENCH
SOCIETY ISLANDS by Marcia Davock.

❑ $12.00   CRUISING MANUAL TO THE KINGDOM OF TONGA IN THE
VAVA'U GROUP (Chart included) The Moorings.

❑ $22.50   AT ANY COST: LOVE, LIFE & DEATH AT SEA (Hardcover)
By Peter Tangvald; thrilling autobiography of a cruising sailor whose
primary home for 50 years was a 49' handcrafted wooden sailboat.

❑ $12.50   SOAP OPERAS OF THE SKY by Jeannie Kuich. A whimisical look at the
soap opera-like tales surrounding the tropical constellations.

❑ $10.00   HOME IS WHERE THE BOAT IS by Emy Thomas. A glimpse into the
cruising way of life.

❑ $14.95   THE NATURE OF THE ISLANDS: PLANTS & ANIMALS OF THE
EASTERN CARIBBEAN by Chris Doyle and Virginia Barlow.

❑ $19.95   CARIBBEAN by Margaret Zellers with breathtaking photos by Bob Krist;
—perfect tropical souvenir or gift.

❑ $25.00   CARIBBEAN: THE OUTDOOR TRAVELER'S GUIDE by Kay Showker;
lots of color photos illustrate flora, fauna & island geology.

❑ $12.95   CRUISING GUIDE TO JAMAICA by Michael and Christine Nunes

❑ $12.95   THE GUIDES TO DIVING AND SNORKELING IN THE BRITISH
VIRGIN ISLANDS or USVI. (Two separate books -- $12.95 Each)

❑ $14.95   THE LEEWARDS, PUERTO RICO, VIRGIN ISLANDS & CHESA-
PEAKE BAY RESTAURANT GUIDES & RECIPE BOOKS (Four
separate books -- $14.95 Each.)

❏ $14.95 SHIP TO SHORE I (A collection of 680 recipes & cooking tips from Caribbean charter yacht chefs) compiled by Capt. Jan Robinson.

❏ $14.95 SLIM TO SHORE (more recipes from Capt. Jan Robinson).

❏ $14.95 SEA TO SHORE (280 seafood recipes and cooking hints.)

❏ $14.95 SWEET TO SHORE (Robinson's ultimate dessert collection).

❏ $10.95 SIP TO SHORE (Robinson's cocktails and hors d'oeuvres collection).

❏ $ 7.95 MAVERICK SEA FARE: A CARIBBEAN COOK BOOK by Dee Carstarphen (Simple shipboard recipes you can prepare at home).

❏ $12.00 **CALENDAR:** THE BRITISH VIRGIN ISLANDS. Photography by Dougal Thornton (New year available in October of preceding year).

❏ $29.95 **VIDEO** (VHS), or (PAL Add $10): SAILING THE WINDWARD ISLANDS by Chris Doyle & Jeff Fisher.

❏ $29.95 **VIDEO** (VHS): ISLAND PORTRAITS: ST. VINCENT & THE GRENADINES by Chris Doyle & Jeff Fisher.

❏ $29.95 **VIDEO** (VHS): CRUISING TRINIDAD & TOBAGO by Chris Doyle & Jeff Fisher.

❏ $29.95 **VIDEO** (VHS), or (PAL Add $10): CRUISING THE NORTHERN LEEWARDS by Chris Doyle & VideoMaster.

WATERPROOF CHARTS

❏ $17.95 U.S. & BRITISH VIRGIN ISLANDS

❏ $17.95 BRITISH VIRGIN ISLANDS

❏ $17.95 UPPER FLORIDA KEYS

❏ $17.95 LOWER FLORIDA KEYS

❏ $ 8.50 CLEAR, WATERPROOF, REUSABLE PLASTIC STORAGE TUBE

— *CALL FOR A COMPLETE CATALOG* —

ORDER FORM VISA MasterCard DISCOVER *(For orders only, call 1-800-330-9542 or 1-888-330-9542).*

To order, check the appropriate box(es), fill out coupon and send check or money order to: Cruising Guide Publications, P.O. Box 1017, Dunedin, FL 34697-1017. Florida residents add 7% sales tax. See schedule for shipping charges. All books are shipped via UPS within 10 days of receipt of order.

SHIPPING & HANDLING:			
	U.S./Terr.	Canada	Other
Up to $15.00	$3.50	$5.50	$7.00
15.01-30.00	4.95	6.95	9.90
30.01-40.00	6.75	8.75	13.50
40.01-50.00	7.75	9.75	15.50
50.01-75.00	8.75	10.75	17.50
Over 75.00	9.75	11.75	19.50
Additional Address Add $3.25.			

$ _____ Total Merchandise

$ _____ Sales Tax 7%
(Florida residents only)

$ _____ Shipping & Handling

$ _____ Total Enclosed

Name _____

Address _____

City _____ State _____ Zip _____

Daytime telephone (_____) _____

(Prices subject to change without notice)